by Michael Miller

A member of Penguin Group (USA) Inc.

To Sherry: It's nice to be social with you.

ALPHA BOOKS

Published by the Penguin Group

Penguin Group (USA) Inc., 375 Hudson Street, New York, New York 10014, USA

Penguin Group (Canada), 90 Eglinton Avenue East, Suite 700, Toronto, Ontario M4P 2Y3, Canada (a division of Pearson Penguin Canada Inc.)

Penguin Books Ltd., 80 Strand, London WC2R 0RL, England

Penguin Ireland, 25 St. Stephen's Green, Dublin 2, Ireland (a division of Penguin Books Ltd.)

Penguin Group (Australia), 250 Camberwell Road, Camberwell, Victoria 3124, Australia (a division of Pearson Australia Group Pty. Ltd.)

Penguin Books India Pvt. Ltd., 11 Community Centre, Panchsheel Park, New Delhi—110 017, India

Penguin Group (NZ), 67 Apollo Drive, Rosedale, North Shore, Auckland 1311, New Zealand (a division of Pearson New Zealand Ltd.)

Penguin Books (South Africa) (Pty.) Ltd., 24 Sturdee Avenue, Rosebank, Johannesburg 2196, South Africa

Penguin Books Ltd., Registered Offices: 80 Strand, London WC2R 0RL, England

International Standard Book Number: 978-1-61564-167-3
Library of Congress Catalog Card Number: 2011941684

14 13 12 8 7 6 5 4 3 2 1

Interpretation of the printing code: The rightmost number of the first series of numbers is the year of the book's printing; the rightmost number of the second series of numbers is the number of the book's printing. For example, a printing code of 12-1 shows that the first printing occurred in 2012.

Printed in the United States of America

Publisher: *Marie Butler-Knight*
Associate Publisher: *Mike Sanders*
Executive Managing Editor: *Billy Fields*
Senior Acquisitions Editor: *Tom Stevens*
Development Editor: *Mark Reddin*
Senior Production Editor/Copyeditor: *Janette Lynn*
Cover Designer: *William Thomas*
Book Designers: *William Thomas, Rebecca Batchelor*
Indexer: *Brad Herriman*
Layout: *Brian Massey*
Senior Proofreader: *Laura Caddell*

Contents

Appendixes

Introduction

Here's the headline:

Social networking is a big deal, and Google+ is the cool new kid on the block. Let me explain.

Social networking has become one of the most common things people do on the internet, second only to searching for stuff. It's all about sharing and communicating with other people—friends, family, classmates, co-workers, and the like. A social network lets you keep your contacts up to speed on what you're doing, and in return you keep up to speed on what they're doing. It's kind of addictive.

The big dog in social networking today is Facebook. I probably don't have to tell you this; chances are you're already using Facebook, to one degree or another. It's that big a deal.

But Facebook has some serious competition, the latest of which is Google+. As you can probably figure out for yourself, Google+ comes from the fine folks at Google. What you might not know, or at least not yet, is what exactly Google+ does.

If I told you that Google+ is a social network, like Facebook, would that help? What if I told you Google+ lets you post messages to your online friends and family? And lets you organize your friends and family into special "circles," and then post messages only to people in a given circle? And offers some really neat and unique features, like online photo sharing, group text and video chatting, and more? Sound interesting?

Well, Google+ certainly sounds interesting to a lot of people. Twenty million of them signed up within the first few weeks of operation (when it was still invitation-only, by the way), and it's been getting rave reviews from those tech types and early adopters who are always looking for the latest thing. It's also been getting some serious looks from regular Facebook users who are fed up with the constant changes on that other social networking site. The general consensus is that Google+ does everything Facebook does (and a little more), but better. I can't say I disagree with that assessment.

Which brings us to the book you're currently holding in your hands. *The Complete Idiot's Guide to Google+* is your guide to everything that Google+ does. I'm guessing you're just starting out with Google+, as we all are, so I'll show you what it does and how it does it. There's a bit to learn, even if you're familiar with other social networks.

Who This Book Is For

The Complete Idiot's Guide to Google+ is written for anyone who is starting to use the Google+ social network. I'm guessing that you have some passing familiarity with social networking, probably through Facebook, but I don't assume that. In other words, we'll start at square one and go from there.

By the way, if you are an avid Facebooker, I place special emphasis on the different ways that Google+ does similar stuff. I also address how best to move from Facebook to Google+, and even how to use the two social networks together, as best you can.

What You'll Find in This Book

The Complete Idiot's Guide to Google+ is your step-by-step guide to sharing and communicating with Google+. While it doesn't have to be read from front to back, it helps if you pick up the initial concepts first before you proceed to the more advanced stuff later in the book.

To that end, I've organized the book into five major parts.

Part 1, Getting Started with Google+ and Social Networking, is a gentle introduction to what social networking is and how Google+ works. This is where you learn how to sign up and start using Google+, as well as personalize your Google+ profile. I also address how best to use Google+ in a safe and secure manner, while keeping your personal privacy in mind.

Part 2, Keeping in Touch with Google+, is all about using Google+ to communicate with friends, family, and colleagues. You'll learn how to find new friends online, how to organize those friends into circles, how to read your friends' posts and make your own, and how to participate in real-time text, voice, and video chats.

Part 3, Sharing with Google+, shows you how to share all sorts of stuff with your friends and circles. I'm talking digital photos, home movies, and interesting stuff you find online.

Part 4, Using Google+ on the Go, addresses how to use Google+ on your mobile phone or tablet. That's right, you can log in and both read and make posts from your iPhone or other smart phone; Google+ actually has a pretty neat little mobile app that's easy to use and quite functional. You'll also learn how to conduct multiple-person mobile text chats, which can be very useful.

Part 5, Doing More with Google+, is for all the advanced users out there. You'll learn how to play social games in Google+, find and use Google+ browser extensions and plug-ins, use Google+ with Facebook and other social networks, get creative with circles and hangouts, and even use Google+ for business.

The Complete Idiot's Guide to Google+ concludes with a glossary of relevant terms and a guide to all of Google+'s shortcut keys. The former is a great place to look up those words and phrases that you've heard but were never sure what they meant; the latter helps you get more efficient use out of Google+.

How to Get the Most Out of This Book

To get the most out of this book, you should know how it is designed. I've tried to put things together in a way that makes learning about Google+ both fun and easy.

In addition to the main text, you'll find a number of little text boxes (what we in publishing call *sidebars*) that present additional advice and information. These elements enhance your knowledge or point out important pitfalls to avoid, and they look like this:

GOOGLE+ INSIDER

These boxes contain additional information about the topic at hand.

GOOGLE+ PLUS

These boxes provide additional tips and advice beyond what's present in the main text.

GOOGLE+ MINUS

These boxes contain important warnings about people and practices to avoid when using Google+.

DEFINITION

These boxes contain explanations of key terms relevant to social networking and Google+.

Let Me Know What You Think

I always love to hear from my readers. Feel free to email me at googleplus@molehillgroup.com. I can't promise that I'll answer every email, but I will promise that I'll read each one!

And, just in case a few mistakes happen to creep into the printed book, you can find a list of any corrections or clarifications on my website (www.molehillgroup.com). That's also where you can find a list of my other books, so feel free to look around—and maybe do a little online shopping!

Acknowledgments

Thanks to the usual suspects at Alpha, including Tom Stevens, Mark Reddin, Janette Lynn, and Marie Butler-Knight, for helping to turn my manuscript into a printed book.

Special Thanks to the Technical Reviewer

The Complete Idiot's Guide to Google+ was reviewed by an expert who double-checked the accuracy of what you'll learn here, to help us ensure that this book gives you everything you need to know about the newest social network. Special thanks to Vince Averello for providing this technical edit of the book—and making sure all the instructions I provide throughout actually work.

Trademarks

All terms mentioned in this book that are known to be or are suspected of being trademarks or service marks have been appropriately capitalized. Alpha Books and Penguin Group (USA) Inc. cannot attest to the accuracy of this information. Use of a term in this book should not be regarded as affecting the validity of any trademark or service mark.

Part 1

Getting Started with Google+ and Social Networking

Just what is this social networking thing, anyway? And what's Google+ have to do with it?

Good questions, and this is the part of the book that answers them. Whether you're new to social networking altogether or a refuge from Facebook or Twitter, I'll get you up and running with social networking generally and Google+ specifically.

In this first part of the book, I'll explain just what a social network is and how Google+ fits into the mix. You'll learn how to sign up and start using Google+ by uploading a photo and building a profile. I'll also show you how to make updates to your profile anytime you like and how to continue your adventure using Google+ safely and securely.

Welcome to the World of Social Networking

Chapter 1

In This Chapter

- Discovering what social networks are
- The history of social networking—from archaic BBS systems to Google+
- How social networking fits into the overall universe of social media
- Speculating on the future of social networking

Google+ is the latest entrant in the world of social networking. It joins Facebook, LinkedIn, MySpace, and a long line of websites designed to promote online social interaction.

Most social networks are similar in what they do, if not how they do it. In this regard, Google+ is no different from its competitors; if anything, Google+ is just the latest iteration of the social networking model that started way back in the 1980s.

What Is Social Networking?

If you're online at all these days, chances are you've heard about *social networking*. Perhaps you're already using a social network, such as Facebook or LinkedIn. Maybe you even saw the movie about the birth of Facebook, *The Social Network*.

DEFINITION

A **social network** is a web-based community that facilitates the sharing of information and experiences between online friends.

But what is social networking, anyway?

Put simply, a social network is a large website that hosts a community of users, and makes it easy for those users to share things with one another. You use a social network to share your thoughts and experiences with others in your social circle. You post everything you want to share in one central location, and your friends can visit that site to see everything you're sharing. Likewise, you can go to that central location to see what your friends are sharing. It's the twenty-first–century way to stay up-to-date with what everyone is up to.

The Elements of a Social Network

To facilitate all this sharing, most social networks offer the following features:

Message posting. You post short text messages (sometimes called status updates) on the social networking site, kind of like mini-blog postings. These messages are typically public for all your friends to read.

Message consolidation. All the messages posted from all your friends are consolidated into a single feed, sometimes called a stream. You can read everything from everyone all in this one place.

Link sharing. You can share links to your favorite web pages in the messages you post.

Photo sharing. You can upload digital photos, typically organized in photo albums, which your friends can then view online and sometimes download.

Video sharing. You can also upload home movies and other videos, which can then be viewed online by your friends. Many social networks also let you embed videos you find on the web, such as those found on YouTube.

Private chatting. Many social networks let you conduct live text chats or instant message sessions with your friends. Some let you do group chats as well—Google+ ups the ante by enabling group video chats.

Interestingly, few of these features are really new to social networking. Most existed previously in one form or another; it took the social networks, however, to piece them together in a way that facilitates a higher degree of social interaction. For example, online message sharing is the same thing you do in a blog, or by posting in a web message forum; photo sharing, of course, is no different from what you do with Flickr or any number of commercial photo upload sites. But social networking gives you all these sharing features in one place, which is pretty useful.

The Rise of Social Networks

While there were elements of social community in the earliest dial-up networks (such as CompuServe and Prodigy) and bulletin board systems (such as The WELL), as well as more recent efforts such as blogs and web-based message forums, the first true social network was Friendster, which launched in 2002 (see Figure 1.1). Friendster not only put together all manner of social features into a single package, it also introduced the concepts of "friends" and "friending" to the internet; it all came from the name, not surprisingly.

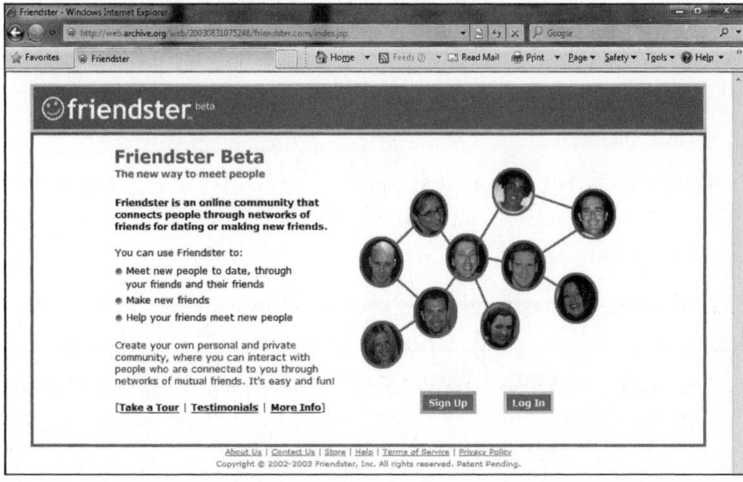

Figure 1.1: *Friendster, the original social network.*

Friendster enjoyed immediate popularity, signing up more than 3 million users within the first few months of operations. That was great, but they couldn't handle the growth and soon ran into major technical problems. (That is, the site crashed a lot—and for extended periods of time.)

GOOGLE+ INSIDER

Friendster eventually survived its technical issues and, under new management, is today one of the largest social networking sites in Asia.

Friendster's technical issues drove users to MySpace, which was then the second-largest social network. MySpace (shown in Figure 1.2) had launched a few months after Friendster, and became the most popular social networking site in June 2006. It remained the top social network for almost two years.

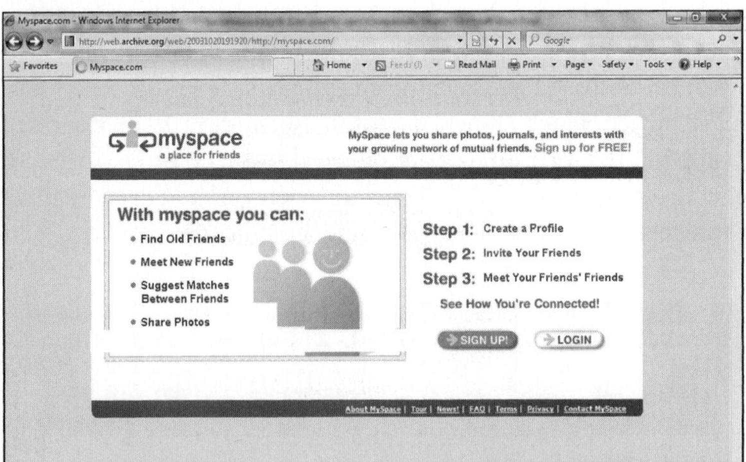

Figure 1.2: *What MySpace looked like back in 2003.*

GOOGLE+ INSIDER

MySpace was acquired by Rupert Murdoch's News Corporation in 2005, and began a long and painful slide into near oblivion. In June 2011, it was sold again to Specific Media, which hopes to revive the site as a hub for music and entertainment.

It seems that 2003 was a big year for social networks. A third major network, *LinkedIn*, was also launched that year. Unlike Friendster and MySpace, LinkedIn targeted business professionals, and became known as a site for career networking. It remains popular to this day, especially in the business community.

A second wave of social networking appeared in 2004 with the launch of a site originally known as "thefacebook," shown in Figure 1.3. What eventually became known as just *Facebook* was originally intended as a site where Harvard students could socialize online. Sensing opportunity beyond that initial market, however, Facebook expanded to other colleges almost immediately, opened its site to high school students in 2005, and then in 2006 let users of all ages (actually, users above the age of 13) in the door.

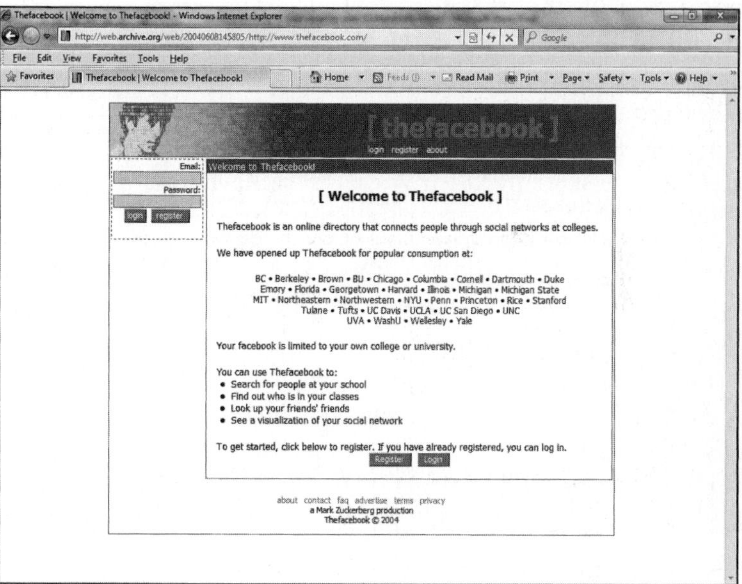

Figure 1.3: *The original home page for Facebook—then called "thefacebook."*

This broadening in Facebook's user base led to a huge increase in both users and usage, with Facebook surpassing MySpace in April 2008 to become the number-one social networking site. Facebook has continued to grow, and today has more than 750 million users.

But that's not the end of the social networking story. Given Facebook's success, other players have attempted to enter the social networking market—which is where Google+ comes in.

Google, not surprisingly, has long eyed the social networking market as a way to extend its dominance in online advertising, as well as a means to expand its online search results. This social networking envy led Google to several ill-fated forays into social media.

First on Google's plate was a true Facebook competitor called orkut, launched in 2004. Similar in features to Facebook, orkut never really caught on, at least in the United States. It's actually a pretty big deal down in Brazil, for some reason, and also has a large following in India. Check it out at www.orkut.com if you're interested.

Next up was something called Google Wave, which was first introduced in May of 2009, and made available to the general public in May 2010. Wave tried to make email more social, cobbling together email conversations and other communications into a single "wave" that could be shared in real time on a collaborative basis. It's a tough concept to explain, which might be why the whole thing was a big bust. Google essentially killed Wave just three months after its public launch.

Then Google came up with the idea of Google Buzz. Launched in February 2010, Buzz was another social messaging tool, this time tied closely into Google's Gmail system. You could use Buzz to share messages privately or publicly; you could also share links, photos, videos, and the like. Unfortunately, Buzz was launched a bit prematurely, before all the privacy implications had been addressed, and Google took some flak for sharing too much information between users' contacts. It certainly did not become the Facebook killer that Google intended.

Finally, Google decided to return to square one and attack Facebook head on—but with some twists. *Google+*, launched on June 28, 2011, is a full-fledged social network, with all the features found on Facebook and other competitors. As you'll learn throughout this book, Google+ tries to do Facebook a bit better, by letting you create "circles" of friends, to better segregate and organize the messages you post and read.

DEFINITION

Google+ (plus.google.com) is Google's most robust offering to date. It's a full-featured social network, offering message posting, photo and video sharing, instant messaging, and more.

It looks as if Google finally got it right. Google+ gained more than 20 million users within its first few weeks of operation, and looks to be the fastest-growing social network in history. It still has a way to go before it overtakes Facebook, but it's well on its way.

Examining Other Social Media

It's important to note that social networking is just a form of a larger phenomenon called social media. Social media are those websites, services, and platforms that people use to share experiences and opinions with each other. That covers everything from the social networks such as Google+ to microblogging services like Twitter.

What kinds of social media are there? Here's the list:

- **Social networks.** As you have learned, these are sites that let users share messages and media with their friends.
- **Social bookmarking services.** A social bookmarking service is a cross-website service that lets users share their favorite websites and online news stories with friends and colleagues online. You visit a website, web page, news article, or blog post that you like, then click a button or link to "like" or bookmark that site. These are great services for spreading timely and interesting content. The most popular social bookmarking services today are Digg, Delicious, and StumbleUpon.
- **Blogs.** A blog, short for "web log," is a kind of personal or professional diary on the web. Most bloggers post information and opinions on a fairly regular basis; some blogs develop a continuing community of commenters on the blog posts.

- **Microblogging services.** A microblogging service is in effect a mini blog, consisting exclusively of short text messages as with Twitter. It's kind of the messaging component of a social network without the rest of the social network; all you get are the short (140 character) messages without any of the surrounding community. Users can subscribe to feeds from individual users, or just search for messages about a given topic.
- **Media sharing sites.** These are sites that let you share media such as digital photos and videos. The most popular photo-sharing site today is Flickr; the most popular video-sharing site is YouTube.
- **Virtual worlds.** These are game-like communities where you interact with other users in graphic fashion via the adoption of an onscreen "avatar."

As you can see, there are lots of different social media, all of which exist to facilitate the sharing of information. Of all these social media, however, only social networks such as Google+ offer the complete package.

The Future of Social Networking

There's no denying that the popularity of social media in general and social networking in particular is increasing, and looks to increase more in the future. As larger numbers of people access social networks on a regular basis, these networks will become a more important hub for people's online activities.

Instead of using individual applications for email, blogging, photo sharing, and the like, people will centralize these activities at a single social network; we're already seeing this. Applications that aggregate information from multiple social media—displaying posts from Facebook, Google+, Twitter, and a user's favorite blogs—will also become more popular, as will applications that make it possible to post a single message to multiple social media.

Also becoming more popular is mobile access—that is, accessing social networks from cell phones and other mobile devices. That's because more and more people are accessing the internet from their mobile phones instead of from their computers. Thus, it's possible to post your status from wherever you might be and be truly social in real time.

The move to mobile connectivity also lets social media become more location based. Social networks will use *GPS* technology embedded in your phones to *geotag* your posts, as well as to inform nearby friends of your presence. With mobile social networking, you can be connected—and social—24/7.

DEFINITION

GPS (Global Positioning System) is a worldwide navigational service enabled by satellite technology. **Geotagging** is the process of adding geographical information to selected items, such as message posts or digital photos.

I'd also look for social networking to become a little more professional in their operation, as the networks themselves mature. You see it already with Google+, which is slicker looking and better organized than its less-professional competitors. (In fact, that's one of the appealing features of Google+.)

As part of this maturation process, I expect social networks to offer more protective privacy options. The days of everyone being able to see everything posted about a person will soon end; users will have an increasing number of privacy options available to hide some or all of their information and posts from unwanted viewers.

And that's a good thing. One of the downsides of social networking has been how easy it is to find private information posted publicly. It's about time that social networks put more restrictions in place to protect their users—and keep private information private.

The Least You Need to Know

- Social networks let you share information and experiences with friends, family, and colleagues.
- Social networks incorporate features found elsewhere on the internet, but in a way that encourages community interaction.
- Early social networks included Friendster, MySpace, and Facebook.
- Social networking is just one form of social media, which also includes social bookmarking services, blogs, and microblogging services (such as Twitter).
- Google+ is the internet's newest social network, but just the latest in a series of social media offerings from Google.

Chapter 2

Introducing Google+

In This Chapter

- What Google+ is and why Google launched it
- Discovering all the things you can do with Google+
- How Google+ differs from Facebook and other social networks
- Why you should use Google+ or switch from Facebook

With the previous chapter's primer on social networking out of the way, we now come to the main subject of this book: Google+. What exactly is Google+, anyway? Should you use it and what for?

I'm guessing you've heard something about Google+, or you wouldn't be reading this book. It's certainly all the buzz of the high-tech circles. So now's the time to take a peek and learn what Google+ is all about.

What Is Google+?

Google+ is Google's new social network. It offers many of the same features and functions as other social networks, such as Facebook and LinkedIn. It's also tied into many of Google's other services, including Gmail and the Google search engine.

GOOGLE+ INSIDER

Google+ also goes by the names Google Plus and G+. For the most part I will stick with Google+, but you will also see G+ in this book.

But what does that mean, exactly?

First off, like all social networks, Google+ lets you share things—lots of things—with other users. More specifically, you share text messages, digital photos, videos, and the like with other members of the Google+ network. It's public sharing, but only amongst Google+ users.

Second, Google+ lets you find out what other people are doing. Again, this is limited to your friends, family, and colleagues who are also Google+ members; you get to see the messages, photos, and whatnot that they share on Google+.

To do all this, Google+ includes a handful of distinct features and functions. These include a "stream" of posts from your friends; the means to organize different "circles" of friends; the ability to text or video chat with one or more people; and even an online photo-sharing service.

In addition, Google+ integrates quite nicely with the rest of Google. You get some nice additions to the Google toolbar when you visit other Google sites; messages from Google+ users show up in your Gmail inbox; and the photos you share on Google+ get stored on Google's Picasa Web Albums site. There's definitely some nice intra-company synergy going on here.

Finally, in case you're wondering, Google+ is free. There's no charge to sign up, and no charge to use it. Doesn't matter whether you sign in once a week or once an hour, your costs are zero.

Why Google Launched Google+

So Google+ is a social network. So is Facebook. So is LinkedIn. So is MySpace. There are a lot of social networks on the web. Big deal. Why, then, did Google decide to get into the social networking thing?

It's all about owning the eyeballs—and the advertising revenue. With the rise of social networking over the past half dozen years, and especially with the growth of Facebook (now 750 million users strong), Google saw a threat to its space on the internet. Even though most of us view Google as a search company, and even though social networking seemingly has little or nothing to do with web searching, Google still viewed social networking as competition. Let me explain.

Google+ Is an Advertising Medium

It helps if you know how Google generates its revenues and profits. While you might think of Google as a search company, it's really an advertising company. Google sells a ton of online ads—on its own search results pages, on the pages of the other online services it offers (such as Gmail, Google Calendar, and the like), and on third-party sites who let Google serve ads on those sites. In fact, Google generates more than 95% of its revenues from advertising; less than 5% comes from licensing its search technology.

What Google is always looking for, then, are new places to sell its ads. That's one of the reasons Google keeps coming up with new products of all flavors; eventually, it can sell ad space on those services.

With this in mind, you can see where Facebook becomes a competitor for Google's ad business. When an advertiser has the choice of placing an ad with Google or with Facebook, Google won't always get the nod. If Google had its own competing social network, however, it then can compete more effectively with Facebook for those advertisers.

So one of the reasons Google created Google+ was to help its advertising business stay competitive.

Google+ Is a Content Generator

In addition, there's a lot of content generated on a social network—facts, opinions, advice, and whatnot, all cloaked as personal posts. Google's main search business is all about collecting, ranking, and delivering content in response to user queries. If Google could add social networking content to its normal web search results, it would deliver more and better search results to users—which, in turn, would help it place more and more expensive ads within those search results.

For the past year or so, Google has tried to work with Facebook to integrate its posts into Google's search results. "Tried" is the operative word; Facebook wasn't that amenable to sharing its content, and Google really couldn't get much without Facebook's cooperation. In fact, Facebook ended up doing a deal with Microsoft's competing Bing search engine, where Facebook status updates are fed to Bing users as part of their search results.

So Google was left out in the cold in regard to expanding its search results with social networking content. What to do next? The answer was simple: start its own social network. Google could then integrate the user-generated content from its own social network into its own search engine. More content, generated from its own users. That's a win-win for Google.

Google+ Is the Latest Thing

I also think that Google wanted to get into the social networking space because it's new and cool. Search used to be new and cool, but that was ten years ago. Google isn't used to being thought of as an "old technology" company, but let's face it, Google is now an established player in the tech industry; the bloom is off the rose, as it were. By entering the social networking space, Google can once again be one of the cool kids at the table, and that always has appeal.

What Can You Do with Google+?

Let's put this all together. Google+ is a social network. As such, Google+ competes directly with Facebook and social networks—for users, advertising revenue, and content.

Fair enough. Now it's time to learn what exactly Google+ does—and what you can do with it.

Google+ Lets You Connect with Friends

Google+ is all about connecting with friends, family, and colleagues. The individuals you choose to connect with are typically referred to as *friends*, although Google rather coldly calls them social connections. I'll stick with friends, if you don't mind.

DEFINITION

A **friend** is someone you interact with on a social network.

Each of your friends (and you, too) create an individual Google+ *Profile*, like the one shown in Figure 2.1. This profile is where you share whatever personal information you want; not just your name and location, but also your education and occupation, likes and dislikes, even your relationship status and "bragging rights." You can share as much or as little information as you like.

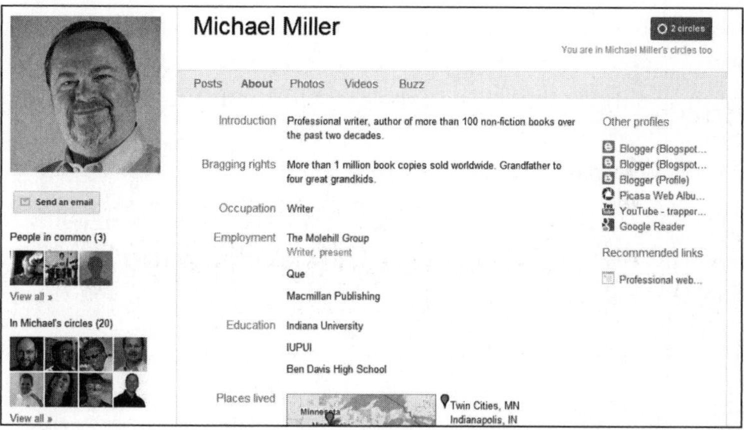

Figure 2.1: *A Google+ Profile.*

To make it easier to share only certain things with certain friends (or to only read posts from select individuals), Google+ helps you organize your friends into distinct groups, called *circles*. A circle is just that, a circle of friends that share some common characteristic. For example, you might create one circle for family members, another for work colleagues, and a third for other parents on your kids' soccer team. You can then send certain posts to your family circle, other posts to your work buddies, and still other posts to the soccer moms and dads. By using the Circles feature, you don't have to send everything you post to every single friend on the network; you can be a little more circumspect, if you like.

DEFINITION

Your Google+ **Profile** contains information about who you are and what you like. A **circle** is a grouping of Google+ friends sorted according to some defined criteria.

Google+ Lets You Share Information

Like Facebook and other social networks, Google+ lets you share information about yourself—facts you find, opinions you hold, things you've done or plan to do. You do this by posting short text messages (called *posts*) to the Google+ site. Each post you make can be read only by those people who you want to read it. When creating a post, you have the option of sending it to specific circles only, or even to specific individuals. Google+ is all about fine-tuning your message distribution; you define who reads a message by the circles you choose to receive that message.

The friends in the circles you choose then see your message in what Google+ calls a *stream*. Your Google+ Stream, shown in Figure 2.2, consolidates all the messages posted by all your friends; you view everything all your friends are sharing, all in one place.

DEFINITION

A **post** is a short text message shared on the Google+ site. The **stream** is where posts from Google+ friends are displayed.

Unless, that is, you opt to filter your stream to display only those posts from friends in a given circle. This is another great benefit of the circles concept; it keeps you from getting overwhelmed from a barrage of posts from people you might not care to hear from today.

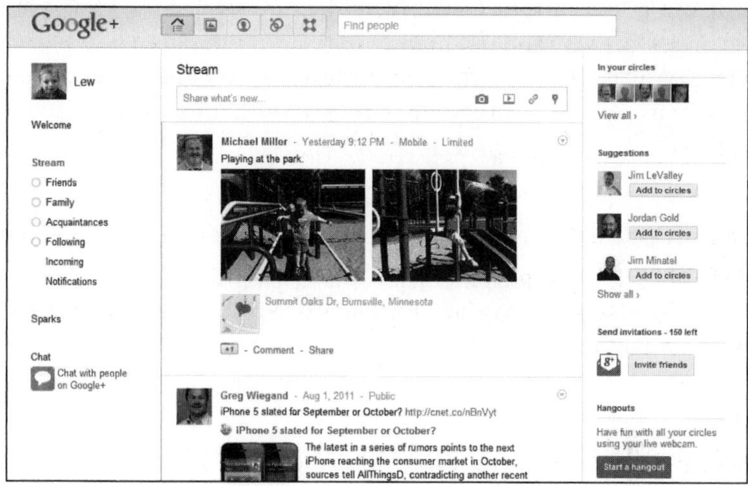

Figure 2.2: *Reading messages in the Google+ Stream.*

By the way, a post doesn't have to be just text. You can format Google+ posts with bold and italic text. You can include links to other web pages in your posts. You can geotag your posts to display your current location. You can even attach digital photos and videos to your posts. In short, you can share just about anything you want to share just by making a simple message post to Google+.

Google+ Lets You Share Photos

Speaking of digital photos, Google+ doubles as a first-class photo-sharing service. Yes, you can attach photos to any post you make, but you can also upload photos into online albums. You can then share your photo albums with your Google+ friends.

You can tag the photos you upload with the names of the people in each photo. This encourages the site's social interaction; photos you're tagged in, even if someone else uploaded them, appear on your Photos page and in your stream. You can also view photos from friends in a specific circle, and they can view photos of you.

Google+ Lets You Chat in Real Time

Social networking wouldn't be very social if you couldn't also communicate in real time with your online friends. To that end, Google+ offers a few different ways to chat online.

First, there's traditional text chat, which lets you do just that in real time with a given individual. This chat feature is built on the Google Talk instant messaging system, so this is another facet of Google+'s integration with other Google services. It works just like any other instant messaging system; you type your messages, your friend types her messages, and your ongoing conversation scrolls in the chat window.

If you're using Google+ on your mobile phone, there's a *messenger* feature that lets you engage in a group text chat. That is, you can text chat in real time with multiple friends.

In addition, Google+ lets you do video chats with its innovative *hangouts* feature. If your computer has a webcam and microphone, you can do one-on-one video chats with other Google+ users, or start up a group video chat with up to 10 participants. You can even broadcast your video chats to hundreds of other viewers in real time, if you like. It's a very cool way to keep in touch with your friends—or even do a low-cost (that is, free) web-based business conference.

Google+ Lets You Play Games

Facebook users can't have all the fun; Google+ also offers a Games section. This is where you can play so-called *social games*, such as Angry Birds, Bejeweled Blitz, and Sodoku Puzzles.

DEFINITION

Hangouts enable multi-user video chat on Google+. **Social games** are online games with social elements—such as the ability to play against other users of a social network. **Messenger** is a mobile group chat service on Google+.

Google+ Lets You Keep in Touch on the Go

These days, more and more users are connecting to the internet not just via their computers, but also via their mobile phones. Google+ offers mobile apps for the iPhone and Android phones, which means you can do pretty much everything you can do while you're on the go. As you can see in Figure 2.3, you can read posts in your stream, write your own posts, share photos, and do group text chats with messenger.

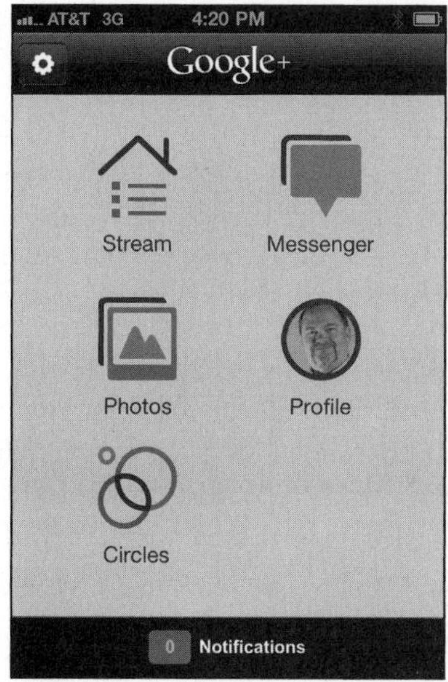

Figure 2.3: *The Google+ iPhone app.*

The mobile version of Google+ is particularly nice for sharing your location. Just select your location from the list at the bottom of the new post page, and all your friends will know where you are. (That's if you want them to, at any rate.)

You can also use G+ mobile to take and immediately share photos with your phone. Just use your phone's built-in camera to take the picture, then tap a button to upload that picture to Google+. It's easy and immediate.

What Really Makes Google+ Different?

Now just about everything you can do with Google+ you can also do with Facebook. To address what makes Google+ different, you need to consider some things I covered in the previous sections.

First, there are a few things that Google+ offers that Facebook and other social networks don't—primarily multi-user text and video chat. These are nice features, but not necessarily significant for all users. The bigger difference between Google+ and other social networks, however, is not in what Google+ does, but in how it does it.

To me, the biggest selling point for Google+ is its "friend management"—the ability to organize your friends into more easily manageable circles. While Facebook does let you organize your friends into friends lists (a recent development, spurred in part by Google+ Circles), it's a feature that's difficult to use and, not surprisingly, little used.

Google+, in contrast, is built around this concept of circles of friends. This drove the development of circles, which is the easiest way to manage large groups of diverse friends I've ever seen. Circles are front-and-center in everything Google+ does, and rightly so.

Speaking of front and center, the Google+ interface is a lot cleaner and more organized than what you find on Facebook, which tends to be a bit cluttered and chaotic—even after that service's most recent interface upgrade. Google+ adheres to the same minimalist design you're used to on Google's search site; you see only what you need to see, and everything else is just a button click away. No more scrolling through an endless feed looking for a given post or wandering around a messy page for the content you need; Google+ offers an orderly approach to social networking.

Behind the scenes, Google+ designers appear to have paid more attention to privacy and security concerns than other social networks. (Are you listening, Facebook?) Google also makes it easy to delete your account and all your data should you want to, which Facebook definitely doesn't.

Finally, Google+ integrates closely with other Google services. When you join Google+, Google adds some Google+ related features to the black navigation bar that appears at the top of all Google pages. It also adds new social networking functionality to services such as Picasa Web Albums and YouTube, which are pretty popular sites. I'd expect to see more of this cross-Google functionality—it's an advantage Google has that Facebook and other social networks simply don't have.

Should You Switch from Facebook to Google+?

Since Facebook has more than 750 million users, chances are you're familiar with that rival social network. How appealing is Google+ if you're a Facebook member—is it worth the effort to switch?

Given that Google+ really doesn't do a whole lot more than Facebook, the initial response might be "no." Unless you really need to engage in multi-user video chat, there's no single compelling thing that Google+ does that Facebook doesn't.

That said, Google+ does offer a much cleaner, more intuitive way to do the things it does. The Circles feature alone might be worth switching for; being able to organize and segment different groups can be a lifesaver if you have a ton of friends online.

Google+ also has appeal if you're a heavy user of Google's other products and services. It integrates well with Gmail, Google Talk, and Picasa Web Albums. Even if you're just using Google search, you get that neat new toolbar that lets you know if you have G+ messages waiting.

Interestingly, some Facebook users have expressed the desire to "start over" with Google+. That is, their Facebook presence has become so cluttered and overwhelming, that the only way to fix things is to start fresh with a new identity on a new social network. Google+ then lets you not only start over, but also start doing things the right way, organization-wise. The only way to fix Facebook, this line of thinking goes, is to abandon it entirely.

Leaving Facebook, however, may not be so easy. A lot of people literally have their entire lives posted to Facebook, in terms of both status updates and other content (photos, videos, and so forth). It's not so easy to walk away from all that, including all your Facebook friends.

It may be that Google+ isn't quite so attractive until some of your friends start to use it, too. Or maybe it's worth being the first to switch, knowing that others will likely follow.

The Least You Need to Know

- Google+ is Google's new social network.
- Google+ offers all the standard social networking features, including message posting and reading, photo and video sharing, game playing, and real-time chat.
- Google+'s unique features include circles (friend organization), hangouts (multi-user video chat), and messenger (multi-user mobile text chat).

Chapter

3

Signing Up and Getting Started

In This Chapter

- Signing up for a Google Account
- Learning how to join Google+
- Discovering the major parts of the Google+ site
- The changes Google+ makes to the Google navigation bar

Anyone can join the Google+ family. All you need is a Google Account (which is free) and to fill in a little information about yourself. From there, it's a simple matter of figuring out how to get around the Google+ site—which is really quite easy.

Signing Up for a Google Account

Before you sign up for Google+, it helps to have your own individual Google Account. A Google Account is a personal user account that provides access to services provided by Google. A Google Account functions as a single logon across all of Google; you need only create a single Google Account to access all Google services, including Google+. (Did I mention that a Google Account is free?)

GOOGLE+ INSIDER

While you can use many Google services, including its main search page, without a Google Account, other services (such as Google+) require you to establish an account and to be signed in to the account in order to use that service. In addition, many Google services provide further functionality when a user is signed in to his or her Google Account. For example, when signed in to your Google Account, you can customize the functionality and results display for Google search.

Creating a New Google Account

To sign up for a new (free) Google Account, follow these steps:

1. Go to the main Google search page at www.google.com.
2. Click the **Sign In** link at the right side of the black navigation bar.
3. When the Google Accounts page appears, as shown in Figure 3.1, click the **Sign Up for a New Google Account** link.

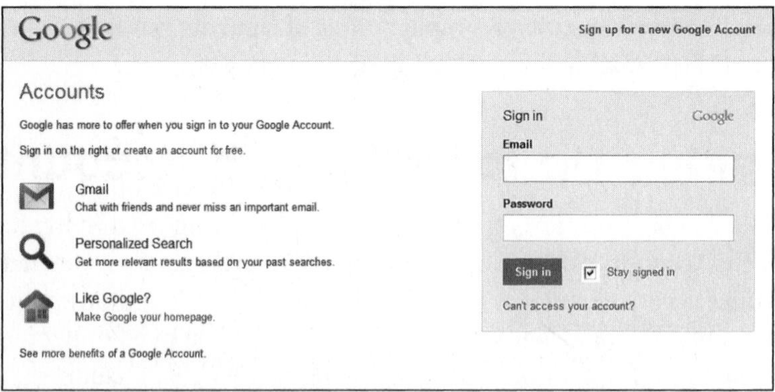

Figure 3.1: *The Google Accounts page.*

4. When the Create an Account page appears, as shown in Figure 3.2, enter your email address into the **Your Current Email Address** box.

Google accounts

Create an Account

If you already have a Google Account, you can sign in here.

Required information for Google account

Your current email address:
e.g. myname@example.com. This will be used to sign-in to your account.

Choose a password: Password strength:
Minimum of 8 characters in length.

Re-enter password:

Stay signed in

Enable Web History Learn More

Default Homepage Set Google as my default homepage.
Your default homepage in your browser is the first page that appears when you open your browser.

Location: United States

Birthday:
MM/DD/YYYY (e.g. "9/24/2011")

Word Verification: Type the characters you see in the picture below.
tonisho
Letters are not case-sensitive

Terms of Service: Please check the Google Account information you've entered above (feel free to change anything you like), and review the Terms of Service below.

Printable Version

Google Terms of Service

Welcome to Google!

1. Your relationship with Google

By clicking on 'I accept' below you are agreeing to the Terms of Service above and the Privacy Policy.

I accept. Create my account.

Figure 3.2: *Creating a new Google Account.*

5. Enter your desired password into the **Choose a Password** box; then re-enter it into the **Re-enter Password** box.

GOOGLE+ PLUS

Your Google Account password must be at least eight characters long. For improved security, use a longer password that contains a combination of upper- and lower-cased letters, numbers, and other characters.

6. If you want to stay signed in across multiple Google services after you sign in to Google+, check the **Stay Signed In** option.
7. To let Google track your usage across its services, check the **Enable Web History** option.

8. If you're using Internet Explorer and want Google as your browser's home page, check the **Set Google as My Default Homepage** option. (This option doesn't appear if you're using Google's Chrome browser.)
9. Click the Location arrow and select your current country.
10. Enter your date of birth, in the form of MM/DD/YYYY, into the **Birthday** box.
11. Enter the generated characters into the **Word Verification** box.
12. Read the Terms of Service, if you wish.
13. Click the **I Accept. Create My Account** button.

Signing In to Your Google Account

Once you've created your Google Account, you can sign in to that account from most Google services, such as the main Google search page. Follow these steps:

1. Go to any Google page, such as plus.google.com or www.google.com.
2. Click the **Sign In** link at the right side of the black navigation bar.
3. When the **Google Accounts** page appears, enter your email address into the **Email** box, as shown in Figure 3.3.

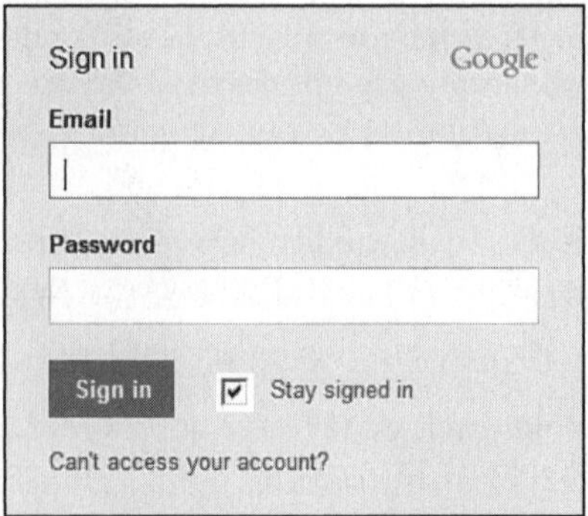

Figure 3.3: *Signing in to your Google Account.*

4. Enter your password into the **Password** box.
5. If you want to stay signed in across other Google services, check the **Stay Signed In** option.
6. Click the **Sign In** button.

Signing Up for Google+

Once you've created a Google Account (or if you already have one), you can then sign up for Google+. The Google+ sign-up is separate from your Google Account, although you sign in to your Google+ account with your Google Account username and password.

Here's how to sign up for Google+:

1. Go to the Google+ home page, at plus.google.com.
2. If you haven't yet joined Google+, you'll see the page shown in Figure 3.4. Enter your first and last names into the **First Name** and **Last Name** boxes.

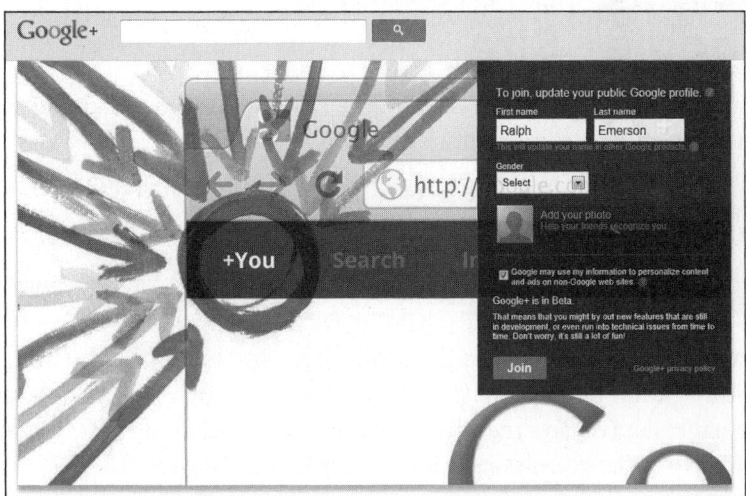

Figure 3.4: *Signing up for Google+.*

3. Click the **Gender** drop-down arrow and select your gender.

4. If you want to add a personal photo at this time, click the **Add Your Photo** link and follow the onscreen instructions. (You can easily add a photo at any time; there's no need to do this now.)
5. If you want Google to use your personal information for advertising purposes, check the **Google May Use My Information** box. Otherwise, uncheck this box.
6. Click the **Join** button.

GOOGLE+ INSIDER

If you already have a Picasa Web Albums account, you may be prompted to link Google+ with Picasa Web Albums. It's to your benefit to do so; click the **Link Google+ with Picasa Web** button when prompted.

That's it. You can now complete your profile and start using the Google+ site. (See Chapter 4 to learn how to complete your Profile.)

Getting to Know the Google+ Site

Google+ is a very easy site to navigate and use. Unlike Facebook and other social networking sites, everything is laid out in a clean and logical fashion—starting with the home page, located at plus.google.com.

Navigating Google+

You navigate from one part of the Google+ site to another by using the navigation buttons that appear at the top of each page, below the normal black *Google navigation bar*. These navigation buttons, shown in Figure 3.5, take you directly to the following pages:

DEFINITION

The **Google navigation bar** appears at the top of all Google pages—the Google search page, Google Calendar, Google+, and so forth—and offers direct access to many popular Google services. You can also go to the Google+ home page by clicking your name (as in **+Name)** in the left side of the black Google navigation bar.

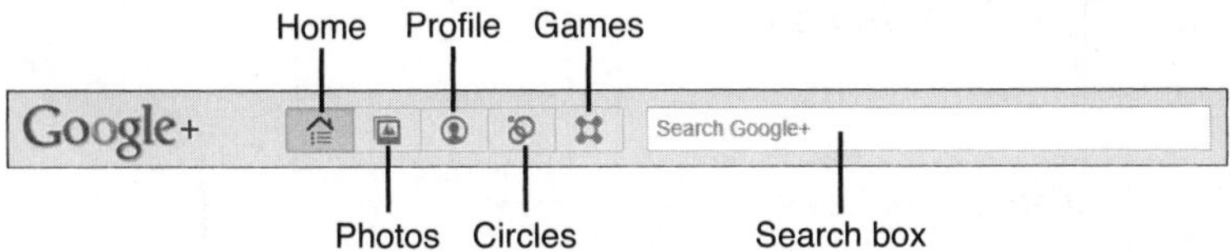

Figure 3.5: *The Google+ navigation buttons (and search box).*

- **Home,** which is where you find the Stream of posts from your Google+ friends.
- **Photos,** where you can view photos from your friends and upload and manage your own photos.
- **Profile,** which displays your Google+ Profile and lets you edit it, as well.
- **Circles,** which is where you can organize your friends into separate groups.
- **Games,** where you can find all sorts of games to play online.

To go to any of these pages, just click the appropriate navigation button.

GOOGLE+ PLUS

Beside the navigation buttons is a search box. It looks like any Google search box, but is used to search for content (and people) on the Google+ site.

Home Page

The Google+ Home page, shown in Figure 3.6, is where you post both your own messages and read messages from others.

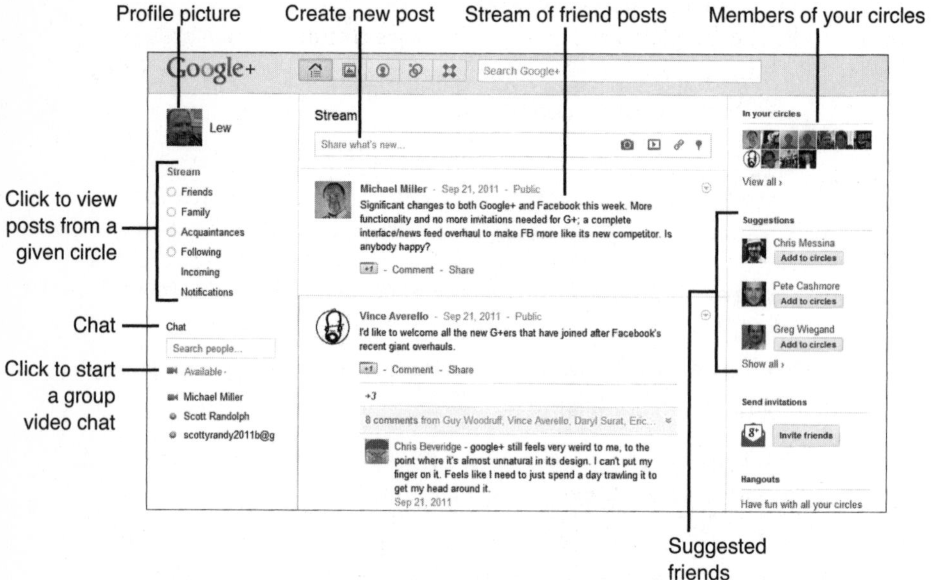

Figure 3.6: *The Google+ Home page.*

The middle part of this page displays the stream, which is a real-time feed of posts made by your Google+ friends. At the top of the stream is a Share What's New... box; this is where you write your own posts that then get displayed in your friends' streams.

The left sidebar on this page contains a variety of useful links:

- At the top of the sidebar is your profile picture. You can click the picture to display your Profile page.
- Click the **Welcome** link to redisplay Google+'s initial Welcome screen.
- Next up is a list of all the circles you've created. Click a given circle to view only posts from members of that Circle, or click **Stream** to view posts from all your friends.

- The Chat section shows which of your friends are online to chat with; click a name to begin chatting.

The right sidebar contains other useful information and links, as follows:

- The In Your Circles section shows thumbnail pictures of some of the friends in your Circles. Click the **View All** link to view all your Circles.
- The Suggestions section contains a list of other Google+ users you may want to add to your friends list. Click the **Show All** link to view all such recommendations.
- The Invitations section lets you invite other friends to join Google+.
- The Hangouts section lets you start a group video chat using Google+'s Hangouts feature.

Photos Page

The Photos page, shown in Figure 3.7, actually has four different views or tabs you can display:

Figure 3.7: *The Google+ Photos page.*

- Photos from your circles
- Photos from your phone
- Photos of you
- Your albums

You change views by clicking the links in the left sidebar. In addition, you can upload new photos to Google+ by clicking the **Upload New Photos** button at the top right of the page.

Profile Page

Your Profile page, shown in Figure 3.8, displays all the personal information you've entered and all the media content you've uploaded. There are tabs, or views, for the following:

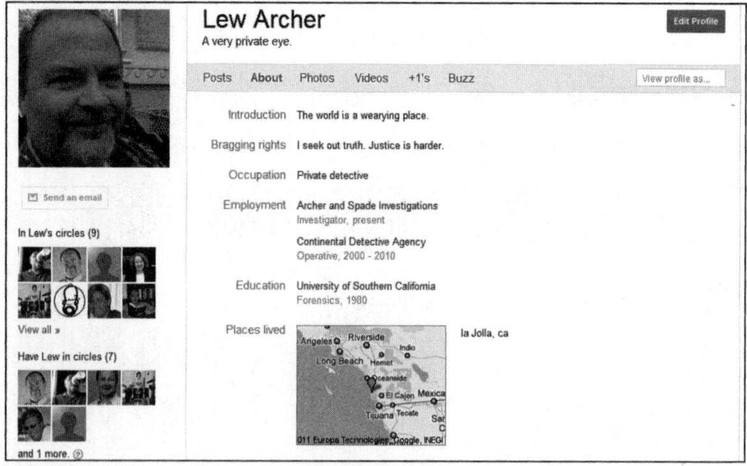

Figure 3.8: *The Google+ Profile page.*

- **Posts:** Displays recent posts you've made.
- **About:** Displays your personal information.
- **Photos:** Shows photos you've uploaded and photos you've been tagged in.

- **Videos:** Shows any videos you've uploaded.
- **+1's:** Displays those web pages you've "liked" by clicking Google's +1 button.

In addition, the left sidebar has a button that lets you send a new email (via Gmail, of course), view everyone in your circles, and view those who've included you in their circles.

Circles Page

The Circles page, shown in Figure 3.9, is where you add friends to your circles—and where you create new circles. You can also manage your circles here, including deleting friends from circles to which they've previously been added.

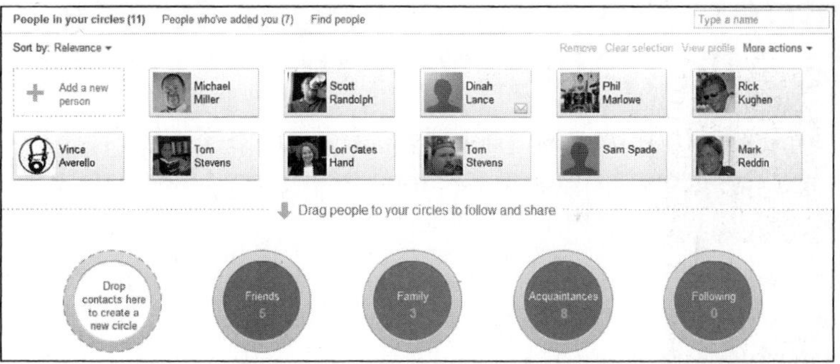

Figure 3.9: *The Google+ Circles page.*

Games Page

The Games page, shown in Figure 3.10, is where you can play online games offered by the Google+ service. These are so-called social games, in that you can play most of them against other Google+ users.

Figure 3.10: *The Google+ Games page.*

Understanding Changes to the Google Navigation Bar

There's one last thing that happens when you join Google+, the Google navigation bar, located at the top of every Google page, changes.

The Google navigation bar has existed for quite some time, but only recently (Summer 2011) in its more prominent black version. The standard Google navigation bar—displayed on all Google-related pages across the web—contains links to major Google services (Web search, Images, Videos, Maps, Shopping, Gmail, and More). It also contains an Options (gears) button you can use to manage your Google Account and other Google settings.

After you join Google+, however, more stuff gets added to the navigation bar (see Figure 3.11). In particular, you see the following new items:

Figure 3.11: *The Google navigation bar, after joining Google+.*

- Your first name, proceeded by a + sign, appears on the far left side of the navigation bar; click this to go directly to Google+.
- If you have any pending Google+ notifications, a red box containing the number of notifications pending appears beside your name on the right side of the navigation bar. Click the red number to view these notifications.
- A Share box appears on the right side of the navigation bar. Click this to create a new Google+ post.
- Your profile picture also appears on the right side of the navigation bar.

These additions to the navigation bar let you continue to use Google+ across Google's family of sites. When you find something that interests you, just make a new post directly from the navigation bar.

The Least You Need to Know

- To join Google+, you first must have a Google Account, which is free.
- Joining Google+ is as easy as entering your Google Account information and filling in a few blanks.
- You navigate the Google+ site by clicking the appropriate navigation buttons that appear at the top of every Google+ page.
- The main pages on the Google+ site are Home, Photos, Profile, Circles, and Games.
- When you join Google+, Google adds several Google+-related features to the Google navigation bar.

Updating Your Profile

Chapter 4

In This Chapter

- Google+ profiles—what purpose they serve and what information they include
- Creating your Google+ profile
- Changing your profile picture

Your profile is how you tell others on Google+ all about you—who you are, where you live and work, what you like, and so on. Your Profile page also hosts all the content you've added to Google+, including the posts you've made, photos and videos you've uploaded, and the like.

It's important, then, that you complete your Google+ profile. You can then edit it at any point in the future, to fill in missing information or update things that have changed.

Viewing Your Profile

You can, at any time, view your own profile on Google+. You'll see exactly what your friends see—which should give you some ideas as to what you need to complete or change.

To view your Google+ Profile, simply click the Profile button at the top of any Google+ page. There are six tabs on your Profile page: Posts, About, Photos, Videos, +1's, and Buzz. Some contain content automatically added by Google+; others require you to submit content.

For the time being, we're interested in the About tab—the one that displays all the personal information you deem worthy to enter.

What's in Your Profile?

When you first join Google+, your profile is somewhat empty. Google fills in any information it knows about you—basically, what you provided when you created your Google Account, or any information added to other Google services. From there, however, it's up to you to complete your profile.

What kind of information can you add? Here's the list:

Introduction. This is a freeform section where you get to write about yourself. You can enter just about anything here; it's the first line most people will see when they look you up on Google+.

Bragging rights. What have you accomplished in life? What are you most proud of? This is where you get to brag about the things you've done, whether that's being an award-winning artist, a top athlete, or just a good dad.

Occupation. What is it you do? What's your career? Enter that here.

Employment. Here you can enter both current and past employers. Filling in this section makes it easier for past and present co-workers to find you on Google+.

Education. Where did you go to college? High school? Even grade school? Enter your school information here to make it easier for old schoolmates to get in touch.

Places lived. Enter the current city where you live, as well as other places you've lived in your life.

Home. If you like, you can enter your home phone number, mobile phone number, email address, fax number, pager number, or chat ID. You can then tell Google who you want to share this contact info with—no one (Only You), anyone on the web, your extended circles (your friends and their friends), your circles, or a custom mix of selected Google+ friends.

GOOGLE+ MINUS

It's safer to not enter contact information, or not share it with others. If your contact information is public, you may be contacted by people you don't want to hear from—even in person.

Work. Enter, if you like, your work contact information, and determine who can see it.

Relationship. Are you single, in a relationship, engaged, married, in an open relationship, widowed, in a domestic partnership, or in a civil union? Or is your relationship status more "complicated?" Enter that here, as well as choose who you want to share it with.

Looking for. Tell your Google+ friends if you're looking for friends, dating, a relationship, or professional networking.

Gender. Let people know if you're male, female, or (believe it or not) "other."

Other names. This is where you can enter other names people might know you by. This is particularly useful for married or divorced women; you can enter your maiden name here to make it easier for old friends to find you.

Nickname. If you're Stephen but everybody calls you Skip, enter "Skip" as your nickname. Again, this makes it easier for casual acquaintances (who might not know your full given name) to find you on Google+.

Search visibility. If you want your Profile to be easily found—that is, if you want it to appear in Google+ search results—enable search visibility. If you want to remain somewhat hidden, don't.

Links. Here is where you list your other pages or blogs on the web.

In addition, your profile can include a picture of yourself, as well as a "scrapbook" of other personal pictures.

GOOGLE+ INSIDER

Your Google+ profile is not just a way for friends to learn more about you, it's also a way for potential friends to find you on Google+. For example, by entering a nickname or maiden name, people searching for something other than your full current name can find you and add you to their friends list. In addition, people often search for others who went to the same school, worked at the same company, lived in the same city, or share the same hobbies or interests. When you enter this information in your profile, people searching in this fashion will be able to find you on Google+.

Completing Your Profile

How do you add this personal information to your Google+ Profile? All you have to do is follow these steps:

1. Log in to Google+ and click the **Profile** button at the top of the page.
2. The first time you access your Profile page, you see the Welcome screen shown in Figure 4.1. Enter any information you wish to add at this point—your profile photo, a tagline (appears under your Google+ name), employment, education, and additional photos to appear in an online "scrapbook."

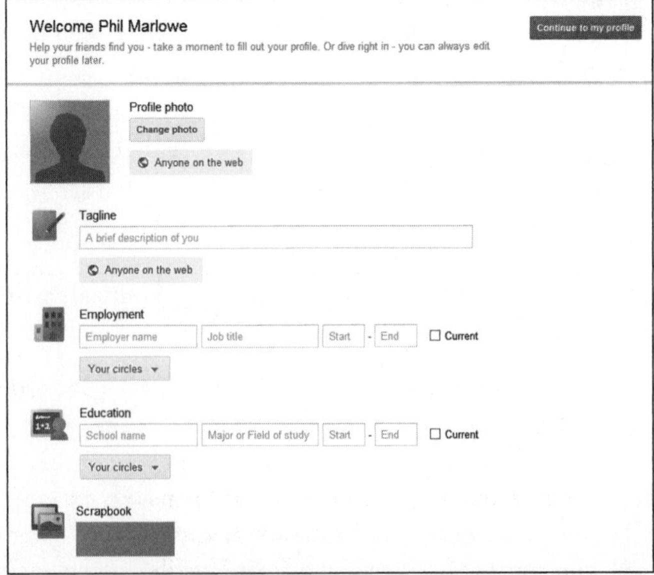

Figure 4.1: *Entering profile information for the first time.*

3. For each item you enter, click the button under the entry box (initially labeled "Your Circles") and select who you want to see this information—**Anyone on the Web**, **Extended Circles** (friends in your Circles and their friends), **Your Circles**, or **Only You**. You can also customize this viewing list by clicking the **Custom** button and then adding individuals.
4. When you're done entering this initial information, click the **Continue to My Profile** button.
5. Google+ now displays the About tab on your Profile page. (This is also what you see when you click the Profile button after your first visit.) Click the **Edit Profile** button.
6. You now see the editable version of your Profile page, as shown in Figure 4.2. Click in any area to enter or edit the information there.

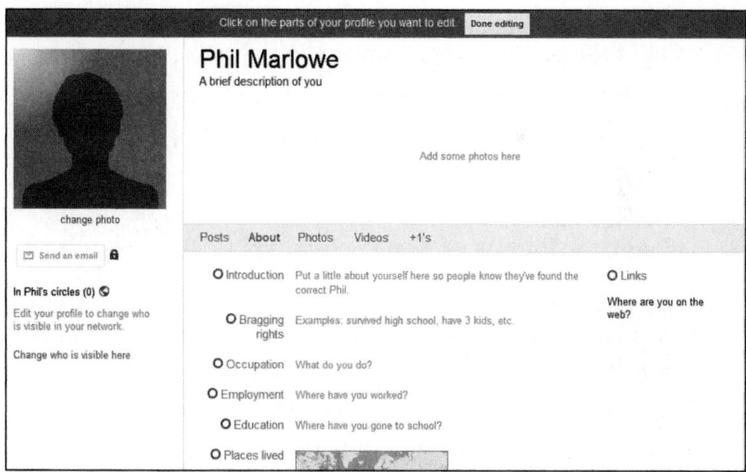

Figure 4.2: *Editing profile information.*

7. When you're done entering information, click the **Done Editing** button at the top of the page.

Your profile is now updated with the new information entered. You can further edit your profile information at any point by returning to your Profile page and clicking the **Edit Profile** button again.

Changing Your Profile Picture

Entering most profile information is as easy as typing it into the entry box. Changing your profile picture, however, is a slightly more involved process, if only because there are several ways to add a picture—you can upload an existing photo, choose a photo from an existing photo album, or choose a photo someone else has uploaded of you.

GOOGLE+ INSIDER

Your profile picture accompanies all the posts you make on Google+, in addition to appearing on your Profile page. Learn more about Google+ privacy settings—in essence, who sees what information—in Chapter 5.

Follow these steps:

1. Go to your Profile page and click the **Edit Profile** button.
2. When the editable version of your Profile page appears, click the **Change Photo** link under the photo or stock image at the top left side of the page.
3. When the Select Profile Photo pane appears, as shown in Figure 4.3, select how you want to choose a photo: **Upload** (from your computer), **Your Photos** (from an online photo album), or **Photos of You** (a photo uploaded by another user).
4. If you choose the Upload option, click the **Select a Photo From Your Computer** button. When the Open window appears, navigate to and select the photo you want to use, then click the **Open** button. When the Select Profile Photo pane reappears, your chosen photo is now displayed, as shown in Figure 4.4. Drag the handles on the corners of the highlighted area to crop the photo, then click the **Set as Profile Photo** button.

Figure 4.3: *Changing your profile picture.*

Figure 4.4: *Cropping your profile picture.*

5. If you choose the Your Photos option, select the album that contains the photo you want to use, then click that photo. When the photo is displayed, crop the photo as necessary then click the **Set as Profile Photo** button.
6. The chosen photo now appears in its place at the top left of your profile page. If you like what you see, click the **Done Editing** button.

You can change your photo at any time by repeating these steps.

GOOGLE+ PLUS

To delete the current profile picture without replacing it, edit your Profile page by clicking the **Edit Profile** button and click the **X** in the top right corner of the profile picture.

The Least You Need to Know

- Your Google+ profile contains all manner of personal information that help your friends learn more about you—and find you online.
- You have to enter most of your profile information manually, which you do by clicking the **Edit Profile** button at the top of your Profile page.
- You can also include a profile picture, which others see on all your Google+ posts.

Using Google+ Safely and Securely

Chapter

5

In This Chapter

- How private information can go public
- Sharing information safely on Google+
- Sending posts only to selected friends and circles
- Configuring Google+'s privacy settings

A lot of people worry about using social networks like Google+ and Facebook. After all, you're putting a lot of your private life out on the public internet, for anyone to see. How wise is that—and does it have to be that way?

The answer, fortunately, is that you have some control over what you post and what others see. This is particularly true with Google+, where you can use the circles feature to send only certain information to selected individuals. It is possible, you see, to keep your personal information private.

How Private Is a Social Network?

Social networking is all about connecting people to one another. That's how Google+ functions, by encouraging you to make lots of online "friends" and share aspects of your life with them.

Google+ wouldn't be much of a social network if it didn't facilitate this type of public sharing of information. That's why most people use Google+, after all, to share things with other people. And, in this context, sharing means making some private information public—at least to some extent.

It gets dicier when you realize that Google itself has access to some or all of the information you share with your friends on Google+. On the plus side, Google uses the information you provide to help you find other friends, and to help them find you. But Google also wants to use your content to feed its search engine and to feed ads back to you. The more Google knows about you, the more targeted search results and ads it can serve—and, if you put a lot of stuff online with Google+, Google can learn a lot about you, indeed.

So here's the question: Do you really want your personal information and posts shared with millions of strangers, with Google and its advertisers, and potentially with hundreds of thousands of unrelated websites that have access to Google's data? I think most people would say no, but this is precisely what Google now does—unless you specify otherwise.

Fortunately, you can configure Google+ to be much less public than it is by default. You can also be a little smarter about the information you post to Google+, and who you let view it.

Sharing Information with Selected Friends and Circles

In Chapter 4, you learned how to add personal information to your Google+ profile. There was a bit there about choosing who could see this information that I admittedly glossed over. Well, that bit is pretty important in maintaining your privacy, so it's worth discussing in more depth now.

Here's the deal: every piece of data you enter on your Profile page has its own privacy settings. That is, for every little thing you enter, you can determine just who can see it—and, by implication, who can't see it. How you configure these settings determines just how private or public you are on Google+.

Naturally, the most privacy can be obtained by not entering any of this personal information—which is the approach some people take. However, you might be comfortable sharing some things with some people but not with others, and you don't need to deprive the chosen just because you don't want to share your information with everyone. Instead, you enter the information but tell Google+ who can see and who can't.

You make this determination when you enter or edit information into your Google+ profile. I won't go into the details of this; revisit Chapter 4 if you need refreshing. But as you can see in Figure 5.1, every entry box has an associated privacy button. Click this button to view the viewing options. Select an option and that particular piece of information will only be displayed to the people you specified.

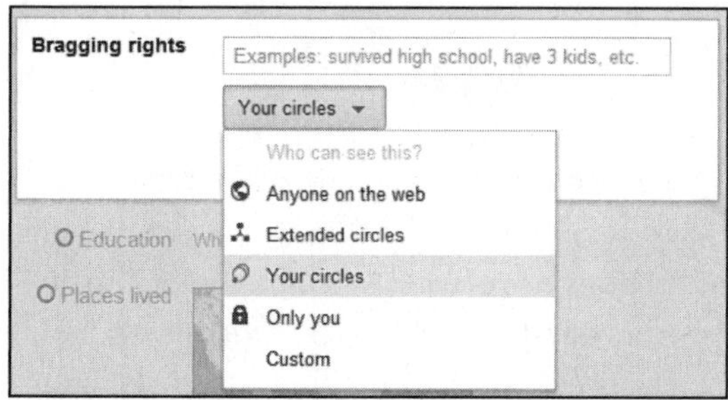

Figure 5.1: *Selecting viewing options for profile information.*

With whom can you choose to share your information? Here are the options:

Anyone on the web. This means exactly what it says—anyone on the web will be able to see this particular profile information. It gets loaded into Google's big index and someone searching for a particular item may see your information in his search results.

Extended circles. An "extended" circle consists of friends of friends. That is, everyone in all your circles, plus everyone in each of your friends' circles, too.

Your circles. This information is visible only to those friends you've added to one of your circles. Anyone not in one of your circles will not see the info.

Only you. This is essentially the "private" setting. You enter the information, but only you can see it. No one else, not even friends and your circles, will see it.

Custom. Select this option if you want to specify individual people who can view this information. When you select **Custom**, you see a pane like the one in Figure 5.2. It's filled by default with Your Circles, although you can delete this by clicking the **X**. You add other people to the approved list by clicking the **Add More People** link; you can then select specific circles to share with, or enter email addresses of individuals you want to see this information.

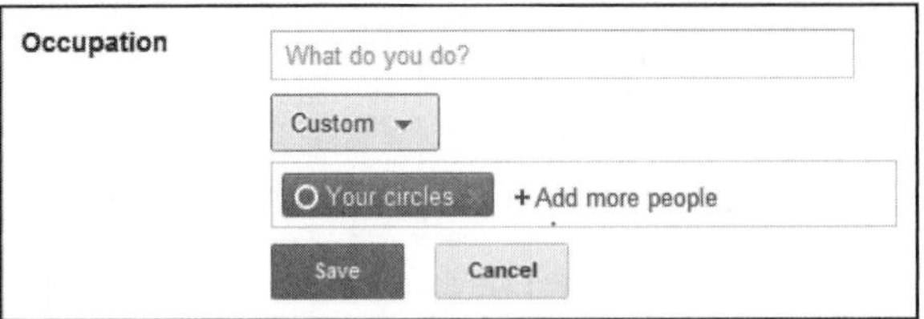

Figure 5.2: *Entering custom sharing options.*

As I said, you can configure these settings for each piece of information in your profile—and each piece of information can be configured separately. For example, you might choose to share your employment information with everyone on the web (so old co-workers can find you), but only share your location information with people in your circles. You choose which information to share with whom.

Sharing Posts with Selected Friends and Circles

People using other social networks often run into problems with sharing too many of their private thoughts. I've heard too many stories of someone complaining about a boss or a teacher or a friend on Facebook, only to have that same individual read the post; as you might imagine, problems ensue. (I've also heard of people in a relationship finding out about their partner's infidelity by reading their Facebook posts.)

The big lesson from this is be careful what you say online; social networks are by nature very public platforms. But it's a little different with Google+, in that it's relatively easy to send posts only to selected groups of friends, not to everyone in the world.

This is due, of course, to Google+'s circles feature. When you make a post, you can choose at that point in time which circles to which it gets sent. That is, you don't have to send every post to everybody; you can select who sees which posts.

How this works is simple. When you go to make a new post, click the **Add More People** link. As you can see in Figure 5.3, you can then:

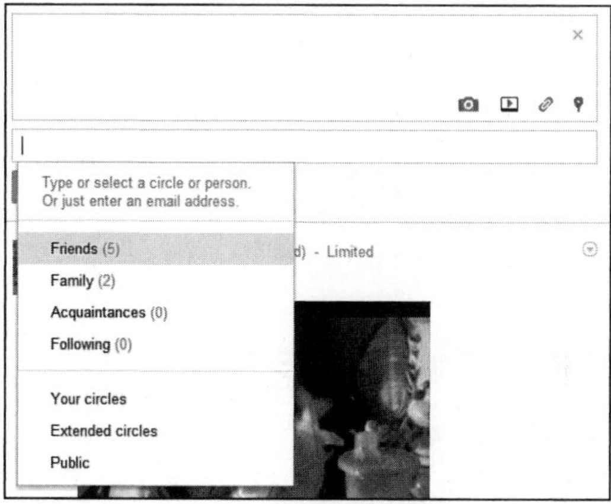

Figure 5.3: *Choosing with whom to share a post.*

- Select a specific circle from the list.
- Choose to share with all circles using the **Your Circles** option.
- Choose to share with friends of friends using the **Extended Circles** option.
- Make the post completely public (this feeds the post into Google's search index).

You can also just enter one or more email addresses into the box. Your post will be sent only to those circles or individuals you select.

GOOGLE+ INSIDER

You can customize and control quite a bit regarding your posts and the stream in Google+. Learn more about posting to Google+ in Chapter 9.

Here's the smart way to use this kind of circle-based posting—create circles for specific types of relationships you have with people. For example, you might create a circle for close family members, another for extended family members, another for work colleagues, maybe another for your bosses at work, and so forth. If you're a student, create one circle for your friends and another for your teachers. Even among friends, you can differentiate your posts; create one circle for your closest friends, another for mere acquaintances—and maybe a third that includes only your boyfriend or girlfriend.

Then, when you post, just select that circle (or those circles) that the post is aimed at. This way you won't end up sending critiques of your boss to your company's management team; send it only to your co-worker or friends circle. It's a great way to keep the various parts of your life walled off from one another.

Examining Google+'s Privacy Settings

Google+'s circles-based posting process makes it easy to share only certain posts with certain people. It also works as a kind of default for future posts; the sharing settings you choose for your last post apply automatically to the next post you make. Naturally, you can change the settings on each post, but defaulting to your last settings is a pretty good start.

That said, there are some other Google+ privacy settings you may want to be aware of. You access these settings by clicking the **Options** (gear) button in the Google navigation bar, then selecting **Google+ Settings**. When the Google Accounts page appears, select the **Profile and Privacy** tab, shown in Figure 5.4.

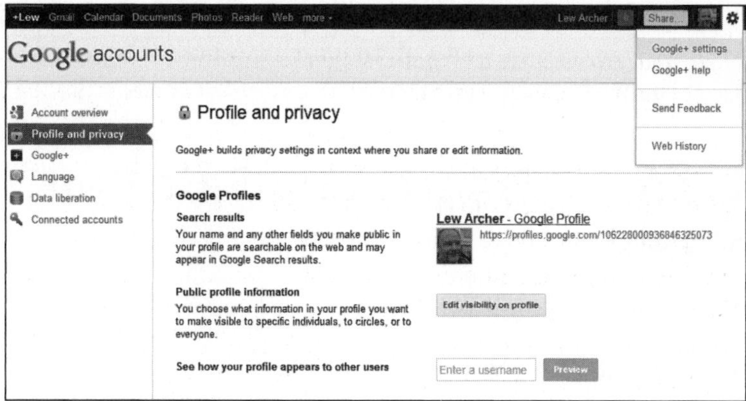

Figure 5.4: *Configuring Google+ privacy settings.*

There are several settings on this page, not all of which directly apply to Google+. (Many of the settings are for your overall Google Account.) Here are the settings to pay attention to:

Public profile information. In the Google Profiles section, click the **Edit Visibility on Profile** button to go to the editable version of your Google+ profile, where you can edit who sees what personal information, as previously discussed.

Network visibility. In the Sharing section, click the **Edit Network Visibility** button to determine who can view the members of your circles. You can limit visibility of each circle's members to others in your circles, or let anyone on the web see them.

Photos. In the Google+ section, click the **Edit Photos Settings** button to configure two important photo-related settings. You can choose to display geotagged location information on the photos you upload, or not; no is the default. You can also select who can tag you in their photos; by default, only those in your circles can tag you, but you can expand this if you wish.

That's not a lot of privacy settings, especially if you're used to the myriad settings in rival Facebook. (Facebook's ever-changing collection of privacy settings will make your head spin, let me tell you ....) The reason why is simple—by default, Google+ keeps a lot of information relatively private. Instead of automatically sharing everything with everybody, Google+ pretty much limits visibility to friends in your circles; it's then easy enough to limit exposure even more from there, if you wish.

Playing It Smart—and Safe—on Google+

So the Google+ designers and engineers took a new approach that allowed for inherent security and user control with fewer settings. That's nice, but all this discussion about configuring Google+'s various privacy settings begs a bigger question—just what should you share on Google+?

How Much Sharing Is Too Much?

In my experience, people share too much information on Google+ and other social networks. People tend to forget that a social network is a public forum, not a private one, and just blurt out stuff they would never think of saying in person. Discretion is undervalued.

That said, it's up to you to determine which information is best kept private, or at least exposed only to your closest friends. The degree of privacy you practice depends to a degree on your personal comfort level and your personal life. But in general, you shouldn't share any information that might prove embarrassing to you or your family, or that might compromise your current job or future job prospects.

Practicing Safe Posting

As I said, what this means in reality is going to differ from person to person. If you work for an ultra-liberal boss, for example, you might not want him to know that you're a teaparty conservative. And if all your friends are born-again Christians, you might not want to publicize that you're really somewhat agnostic.

But it goes further than that. If you're preaching the "just say no" drug message to your kids, you might not want to list *Harold and Kumar Go to White Castle* as one of your favorite movies (even though it is hilarious); it might compromise your integrity on the matter just a bit. For that matter, you might want to hide all those photos that show you knocking back some cocktails at your friends' beach party, for both your kids' sake and to ward off any awkward questions from teetotalling employers.

The same goes with the messages you post on Google+. There are stories, some of them true, of careless (and carefree) employees posting from the local watering hole when they were supposed to be home sick from work. Employers can and will keep track of you online, if you're stupid enough to post all your comings and goings.

GOOGLE+ MINUS

Don't assume that limiting posts to select circles will totally protect you. It's all too easy for a friend in a circle to share what you post with his friends—who may know someone else who can get you in trouble. Just assume that if you post something on the internet, even to a limited group of people, it can and probably will go public.

It's not just the factual stuff that can get you in trouble, either. Spouting off your opinions is a common-enough social networking activity, but some people are bound to disagree with you or take more serious offense. Do you really want to start an online flame war over something you posted in haste?

For that matter, it's a really bad idea to use Google+ to criticize your employer, the people you work with, your teachers, or just people you associate with in the community. Posting about how much you hate your job will eventually get back to your boss, even if you complain only to your nonwork friends. The resultant discussion will not be pleasant.

As I said, discretion is the way to go. When in doubt, just don't post it or upload it. It's okay to keep some thoughts to yourself; you don't have to post every little thought that enters you mind. Really, you don't.

How Much Do Your Friends Really Need to Know?

The same goes with your contact information. Do you really want complete strangers to know where you live, where you're at this moment, or your phone number? I certainly don't. It may seem innocuous to post that you're having a nice weekend getaway with your spouse, but if you've included your home address in your Google+ profile, that's an invitation for someone to rob you blind.

Again, it's better to be discrete, and not tell everyone how to contact you. If someone does want to contact you, they can send you a message on Google+; that's pretty safe. They don't have to be able to contact you via email, ring you up on the phone, or show up on your doorstep. There are too many nutcases out there not to be careful.

Bottom line, then, is this: be careful about the information you post to Google+. It's better to keep most of your personal information private—and make it not so easy for unwanted people to contact you.

GOOGLE+ MINUS

Everything just mentioned applies not only to yourself, but also to your kids when they use Google+. In fact, youngsters tend to be very open about their lives online, when they should be practicing more discretion. You should monitor your children's use of Google+, to make sure they're not putting more information out there than they should.

The Least You Need to Know

- Anything you post online can become public; dumb posts that fall into the wrong hands can be very embarrassing.
- Google+ lets you share information and posts only with selected circles and friends.
- Even with Google+'s selective posting, you should always practice discretion when posting information and messages.

Keeping in Touch with Google+

Part 2

The main reason people enjoy using social networks is to connect with others. Google+ lets you communicate with family, friends, colleagues, or whomever you like, just like other social networks, but with some new and interesting twists. The more you know about these new features, the more you can enjoy using Google+.

In the next few chapters, I'll explain how to find friends and use Google+'s unique features to keep in touch with them. Perhaps you have already heard about circles, streams, and hangouts, but just what are these things, anyway? Well, circles is a way to organize your Google+ friends; the stream is where you read and comment on all your friends' posts; and a hangout is how you chat with multiple friends in real time, via video. Got it?

Finding Friends

Chapter

6

In This Chapter

- Understanding what Google+ friends are
- Adding friends with Google accounts
- Finding friends using Yahoo! Mail, Hotmail, and other email services
- Inviting a person to join you on Google+

Google+ is all about connecting with friends, family, and colleagues. The question is, where do you find friends to connect with?

There are many ways to find friends on Google+. You can also invite friends outside of Google+ to join the network. All it takes is a little online legwork.

Understanding Google+ Friends

What Google+ calls "social connections," the rest of us call "friends." A friend (or a social connection, if you insist) is someone you connect with on Google+ and add to one or more of your circles.

Once someone is your friend on Google+, you can share lots of things with them. When you make a post, your friend sees your post in his stream. You can also share links, photos, and videos with your Google+ friends, as well as any web pages you like. You can also include your friends in texts and video chats.

GOOGLE+ INSIDER

A Google+ circle is merely a collection of friends that share some characteristic, organized into a single group. Learn more about circles in Chapter 7.

It's easy to add friends to your Google+ network. In fact, there are several ways to do it, depending on where your potential friends are.

Finding Friends on Google+ and Gmail

The first place to look for friends is on Google. Specifically, anyone who already has a Google+ or Gmail account is known to Google, and thus easy to find.

Finding Friends—the Fast Way

There are actually several ways to find new friends who have Google+ or Gmail accounts. Here's the fastest and easiest way to do it:

1. Click the **Circles** button at the top of any Google+ page.
2. When the circles page appears, as shown in Figure 6.1, click the **Add a New Person** box.

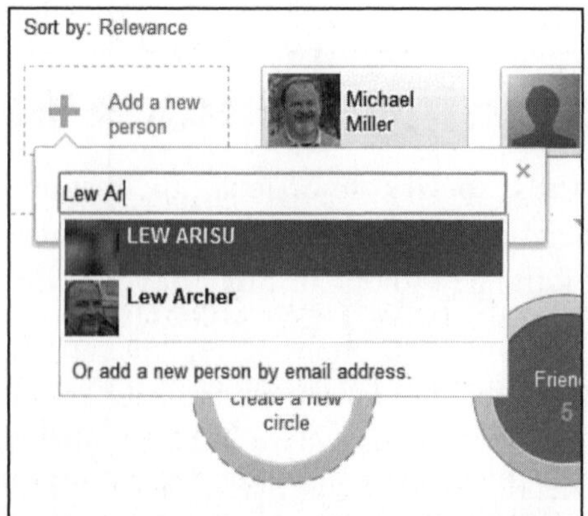

Figure 6.1: *Searching for friends on the circles page.*

3. The box now expands to include a search box. Start typing the name of the person you want to find in this box.
4. As you type, Google will suggest people who match your query. Select your friend's name from this list.
5. You are now prompted to add this person to one of your circles, as shown in Figure 6.2. Select a circle or click the **Create New Circle** link to add this person to a new circle.

GOOGLE+ PLUS

You can add a person to more than one circle.

6. Click **Save** when done.

Figure 6.2: *Adding a person to a circle.*

Your new friend is now added to the chosen circle.

Finding More Friends on Google

While the previous method is fast and easy, it doesn't provide a complete list of people who match your query—just a short list based on people you know. You can, however, display a more complete list of Googlers to friend by following these steps.

1. From the top of any Google+ page, enter the person's name in the **Find People** box, then press **Enter**.
2. Google now displays a list of people who match your query and have Google profiles, as shown in Figure 6.3. To read a person's profile, click their **Google Profile** link.

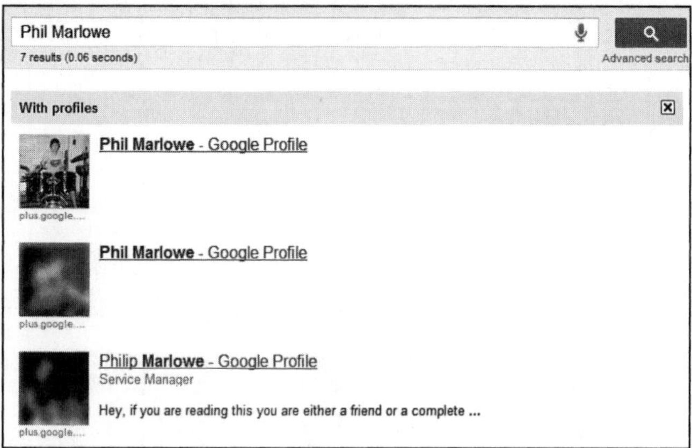

Figure 6.3: *Potential friends who match your search.*

3. Once that person's profile page is displayed, you can then add them to your friends list. Just click the **Add to Circles** button and then select the circle (or circles) to add them to, as shown in Figure 6.4.

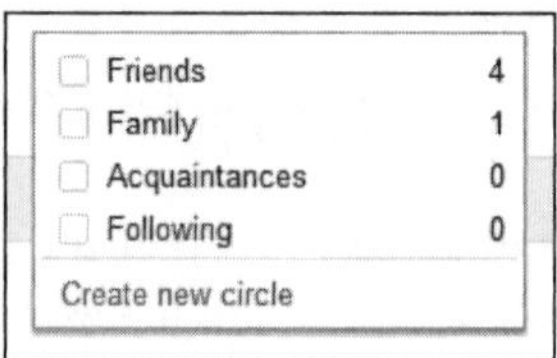

Figure 6.4: *Adding a friend to a circle.*

Letting Google Recommend Friends

Not surprisingly, Google will also recommend friends to you. These are folks that either appear in your Gmail contacts list or who are friends of existing Google+ friends. You might find these recommendations useful, or not.

To view these recommendations, follow these steps:

1. Click the **Circles** button at the top of any Google+ page.
2. When the circles page appears, click the **Find People** link.
3. Google now displays its recommendations, as shown in Figure 6.5. (There are actually more people listed than you can see on a single screen; scroll down to view additional suggestions.) To add a person to a circle, simply drag that person's box into a circle below.

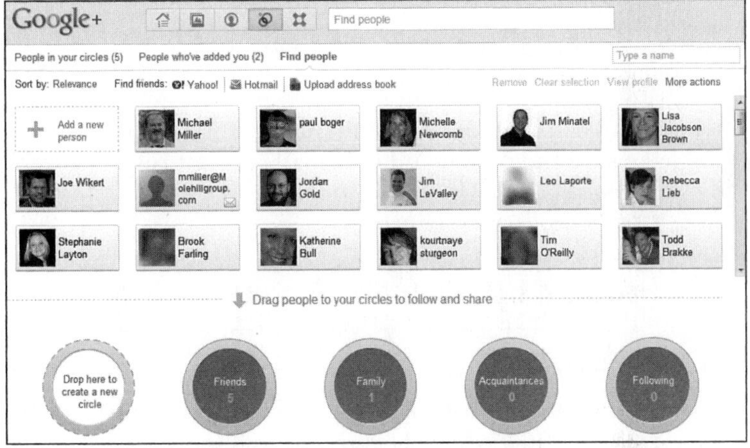

Figure 6.5: *Viewing Google+'s friend recommendations.*

Finding Other Email Friends

Google+ can also import contacts from other email services, and you can invite these folks to join Google+ and be your friends. You can import contacts from Yahoo! Mail, Hotmail, and many desktop email programs, including Microsoft Outlook, Mozilla Thunderbird, and the Apple Address Book.

GOOGLE+ INSIDER

You can import contacts from any address book that can export data in comma separated value (.CSV) or vCard (.VCF) formats—which are offered by most spreadsheet and address book programs.

Finding Friends from Yahoo! Mail

Let's start by importing and inviting friends from your Yahoo! Mail contacts list. Follow these steps:

1. Click the **Circles** button at the top of any Google+ page.
2. When the circles page appears, click the **Find People** tab.
3. In the Find Friends section, shown in Figure 6.6, click the **Yahoo!** link.

Figure 6.6: *Finding other email friends.*

4. When the Yahoo! window opens, as shown in Figure 6.7, make sure the correct Yahoo! email account is selected, then click the **Agree** button.

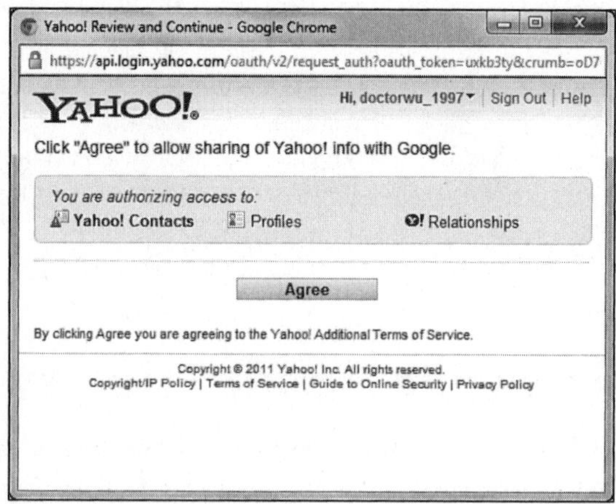

Figure 6.7: *Connecting your Google+ account to your Yahoo! account.*

5. Your Yahoo! contacts now appear on your circles page, as shown in Figure 6.8. Drag any contact onto a circle to add that person to the circle.

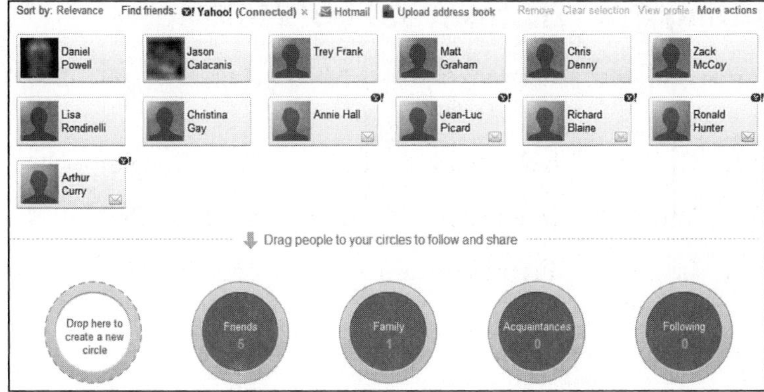

Figure 6.8: *Yahoo! contacts on your Google+ Circles page.*

Any person you add to a circle will receive an invitation (via email) to join Google+. When that person responds in the affirmative, he or she will officially be added to your circles.

GOOGLE+ PLUS

If you're a Facebook member, you'd probably like to import your Facebook friends into Google+. Unfortunately, there's no official way to do that; Google does not allow you to directly import Facebook friends into Google+. You can, however, import your Facebook friends into a Yahoo! Mail account, and then import those friends from Yahoo!, as described here. It's a bit of a workaround, but it works—and I describe it in full detail in Chapter 19.

Finding Friends from Hotmail

If you're a Hotmail subscriber, it's equally easy to add your Hotmail contacts to your Google+ circles. Follow these steps:

1. Click the **Circles** button at the top of any Google+ page.
2. When the circles page appears, click the **Find People** tab.
3. In the Find Friends section, click the **Hotmail** link.
4. When the Connect to Messenger window opens, as shown in Figure 6.9, enter your Windows Live ID (typically your Hotmail address) and your password, then click the **Connect** button.

Figure 6.9: *Connecting your Google+ account to your Windows Live (Hotmail) account.*

5. Your Hotmail contacts now appear on your circles page. Drag any contact onto a circle to add that person to the circle.

As with Yahoo! contacts, any Hotmail contact you add to a circle will receive an invitation (via email) to join Google+. When that person responds in the affirmative, he or she will officially be added to your circles.

Finding Friends in Your Email Address Book

If you use a desktop email program, such as Microsoft Outlook, you can import your contacts from that address book into Google+, and then send invitations to selected contacts to join your circles. It's a slightly more complicated process that goes like this:

1. Click the **Circles** button at the top of any Google+ page.
2. When the circles page appears, click the **Find People** tab.

3. In the Find Friends section, click the **Upload Address Book** link.
4. When the Open Dialog box appears, navigate to and select your email address book file, then click the **Open** button.

GOOGLE+ INSIDER

You may first need to export contacts from your address book into a comma separated value (.CSV) or vCard (.VCF) format file. See the instructions for your particular email program on how to do this.

5. Your email contacts now appear on your circles page. Drag any contact onto a circle to add that person to the circle.

Any contact you add to a circle will receive an invitation (via email) to join Google+. When that person responds in the affirmative, he or she will officially be added to your circles.

Inviting Non-Google+ Friends to Join Up

What if you want to friend someone who isn't signed up for a Google service and doesn't exist as a contact in any of your email programs or services? Well, Google+ lets you invite anyone manually to join your circles—as long as they have an email address.

Follow these steps:

1. Click the **Circles** button at the top of any Google+ page.
2. When the circles page appears, click the **Add a New Person** box.
3. The box now expands to include a search box. Enter the person's email address into this box, then press **Enter**.
4. You are now prompted to add this person to one of your circles. Select a circle or click the **Create New Circle** link to add this person to a new circle.
5. Click **Save** when done.

This person will now receive an email invitation to join Google+. When that person responds in the affirmative, he or she will be officially added to the specified circle(s).

Deleting Friends

Over time you may find that you've added people as friends who you're no longer friendly with. Fortunately, it's easy to remove friends from Google+. Just follow these steps:

1. Click the **Circles** button at the top of any Google+ page.
2. When the circles page appears, click the **People in Your Circles** tab. This displays all your Google+ friends.
3. Click the friend you want to remove. Note, you can select multiple people if you like.
4. Click the **Remove** link above the list of friends.

The selected friend will now be globally removed from all your circles. (You don't have to remove them from each circle individually.)

The Least You Need to Know

- A friend, or social contact, is someone you share things with on Google+.
- To become your friend on Google+, a person must be added to one or more circles.
- You can find new friends by searching people with Google+ or Gmail accounts, importing contacts from your email address book, or inviting someone directly via email.
- Google+ also recommends people it thinks might make good friends; these are typically people in your Gmail contacts list, or friends of people who are already your friends.

Working with Circles

Chapter 7

In This Chapter

- Discovering Google+'s unique circles feature
- Managing your social connections with circles
- Creating a new circle
- Adding friends to circles
- Posting to your circles

One of the most talked-about features of Google+ is circles. In fact, it's really how Google+ is built, around the concept of circles of friends. Instead of dumping all your friends into one giant bucket (the traditional Facebook model), you instead group similar friends into several smaller buckets that Google calls circles. You can then send your posts only to those in specific circles; you can also filter your reading so that you only see posts by friends in selected circles.

It sounds fairly simple on paper, and in fact it is quite easy to start organizing your friends into circles. But how best can you use circles to simplify your social networking? Read on to find out.

Understanding Circles

To understand Google+, you must understand the concept of circles. The whole circles thing is a way of thinking about social interactions, a way of organizing your friends, and a way of isolating what you share. It's what Google+ is built around. If you've used Facebook or other social networks at all, you're used to a different way of organizing your social interactions—essentially, no organization at all. When you make a post on Facebook, for example, it gets sent to every single friend on your friends list. Your Facebook News Feed (Facebook's version of Google+'s Stream) displays posts from every single friend you have. Everybody is connected to everybody else, and everybody sees everything. It's total chaos, and if you have more than a few dozen friends, eventually it can become overwhelming.

GOOGLE+ INSIDER

Faced with this new competition, Facebook recently copied Google+ by adding their own version of circles, called friends lists. While these friends lists mimic circles in theory, they're really just an add-on to Facebook's inherently chaotic approach, and much harder to implement in reality. (In fact, most Facebook users don't use them or like them that much.)

The staff of Google+ recognized this inherent failure of the traditional social networking model, and decided to go about it in a slightly different way. Yes, social networking is all about sharing and building communities, but that doesn't mean that everybody wants to share everything with everyone. The Googlers eventually came round to the concept of circles of friends—that is, the fact that all of us, in the real world, maintain multiple groups of friends. Why shouldn't we behave the same way online?

If you're like me, you don't hang out with a massive group of friends and do everything with the entire group. No, you segment your friends into like groups, and hang out with each group individually. Oh, you may have a few friends who bridge two or more groups, but in general the streams don't cross.

For example, in the real world you may have relationships with your spouse and kids; with your parents and siblings; with your cousins, aunts, and uncles; with your colleagues during work hours; with different co-workers after work; with members of a softball or volleyball team; with members of a book club or other hobbyist group; and with your neighbors down the street. You don't have the same conversations with every one of these groups; you wouldn't send them all the same letter or email message.

When you start using Google+, you can work with Google+'s default circles—Friends, Family, Acquaintances, and Following. Now, that's a good start on how you might segment your social interactions, but you can go beyond that and create your own custom circles. So you might add circles for Extended Family, Business, After Work Friends, Softball Team, Book Club, Neighbors, and the like.

And here's the great thing. Every time you make a post on Google+, you determine which circle (or circles) receive that post. So if you want to talk about a family matter, post it only to your Family circle. If you want to josh about with your closest pals, post it to the Friends circle. If you have a business matter to discuss, post it to your Business circle. If you have a question about an upcoming softball game, post it to the Softball Team circle. You get the picture.

Likewise, you can choose to read posts only from members of a certain circle. Maybe you prioritize family matters and read the Stream from your Family circle every day. Maybe keeping in touch with your neighbors is less important, so you read your Neighbors stream only once a week. You don't have to get overloaded with posts from hundreds of people; you can read only those posts from those circles that matter to you at the moment.

GOOGLE+ INSIDER

By default, Google+ offers a Following circle, which is similar to the way following works on Twitter. When you add someone to your Following circle, you get to read their public posts, but they don't see the posts you make.

Why Circles Are Special

What I like about Google+'s circles are that they mirror how we interact with friends and family in real life. Not all friends know everything about us, nor do we participate in all aspects of our friends' lives. Our relationships are not all of the same depth; relationships are complicated.

Real-world relationships are not necessarily symmetric, either. That is, you may consider a person your very best friend, but that person may think of you only as a good friend, not their bestie.

Google+, through its use of circles, comes close to reflecting this type of relational nuance. Other social networks, Facebook and Twitter included, do not. I can't tell you how many complaints I've had from Facebook users that they're pretty much forced to deal with all their online "friends" at the same level; there's no convenient way, on Facebook, to view some friends as more important or just different from others.

At least Google+ gets the organizational aspects of relationships right. If you set up your circles early and thoughtfully, and are diligent about using circles to organize your friends, you should experience a more natural form of social interaction than you do with Facebook and other social media. It's a smart way to interact with people online.

How Google+ Circles Work

Now, for some details on how circles work. It's pretty much the same way you define circles of friends in the real world, but with some practical rules.

First, know that Google+ lets you create as many circles as you like; there's no limit. You don't have to be confined to the four default circles (Friends, Family, Acquaintances, and Following) that Google+ defines for you. You can create circles around any topic or type of relationship you want.

GOOGLE+ INSIDER

While you can create an unlimited number of circles, Google+ does limit you to 5,000 friends total.

When you make a friend on Google+, he or she has to be assigned to a circle—if a contact isn't in a circle, you don't have a relationship with that person. That said, you can add any person to any circle, and even add the same person to multiple circles. Just as your real-world friends sometime overlap social groups, your online contacts can occupy more than one circle at the same time.

It's also important to realize that the whole circle thing is a way of organizing things for you, but doesn't force the same organization on others. Just because you add someone to one of your circles doesn't mean they've added you to one of theirs.

GOOGLE+ INSIDER

Google+ Circles defines one-way relationships. In this fashion, Google+ is more like Twitter, where someone can follow you without you following them, unlike Facebook where you have to mutually agree to "friend" each other.

It works the other way, too—other Google+ users can add you to their circles, and they don't need your permission to do so. However, you can block people from circling you, if you wish. It's safe to do this, as Google+ won't notify the other party that you've blocked them.

By the way, a person doesn't have to be a Google+ member to be added to your circles. You can add nonmembers by their email addresses; they'll receive your posts via email until they decide to sign up for Google+ on their own.

When you post an update to Google+, you use circles to determine who sees the post. While you can post truly public messages that can be viewed by anyone, it's more in keeping with the segmented approach that you post only your message to selected circles. You can opt to post to all circles, selected circles, extended circles (people who are in the same circles that the friends in your circles are in), or just to specific individuals, regardless of their circle connection. (You can also opt to make a post public, meaning that it's visible to anyone who has you in a circle.)

When you want to read updates, you have the choice of viewing your entire stream (everyone in all your circles), or just viewing those posts from people in a particular circle or group of circles. It makes the process of keeping up to date a little easier.

Creating a New Circle

Now it's time to get down to circular business. As previously noted, Google+ comes preconfigured with four somewhat generic circles:

- Friends
- Family
- Acquaintances
- Following

You can use these four circles to classify your friends, or you can create additional custom circles that have more meaning to you. Here's how you create a new circle:

1. Click the **Circles** button at the top of any Google+ page.
2. When the circles page appears, as shown in Figure 7.1, hover over the circle on the left that says **Drop Here to Create a New Circle**. The text in this circle now changes to read **Create Circle**.

Figure 7.1: *Getting ready to create a new circle from the circles page.*

3. Click the **Create Circle** circle.
4. Google+ now displays the dialog box shown in Figure 7.2. Enter the name for this new circle into the first text box.

Figure 7.2: *Creating a new circle.*

5. If you want to add a description for this circle, click the **Click to Add a Description** link. This opens a new text box; enter a short description here.
6. To add a person to this circle now (you can wait until later, if you like), click **Add a New Person**, then enter that person's name or email address.
7. To create the circle, click the **Create Empty Circle** or **Create Circle with *X* Persons** button. (Which button you see depends on how many people—if any—you added to the circle at this point.)

The circle is now created and added to your circles page.

Assigning Friends to Circles

Of course, a circle isn't very useful until you add some people to that circle. What happens, then, when you add someone to a circle?

First, you can share posts and other items with that person, and you can see what he's sharing with you.

Second, he'll be notified that you've added him to one of your circles and be able to add you to his circles, if he wants. Know, however, that when you add someone to a circle, that person never sees the name of the circle; feel free to add someone you don't really like to a "Nimcompoop" circle, if you like.

Finally, the person you add to a circle will appear in the list of friends on your profile page.

Here's how to add people to circles:

1. Click the **Circles** button at the top of any Google+ page.
2. When the circles page appears, select the group of people you want to choose from: **People in Your Circles**, **People Who've Added You**, or **Find People**.

GOOGLE+ PLUS

Use the **Find People** tab on the circles page to find likely friends, or to search for potential friends (using the search box at the top left corner).

3. Find the person you want to add, then drag and drop that person's name onto the desired circle, as shown in Figure 7.3.

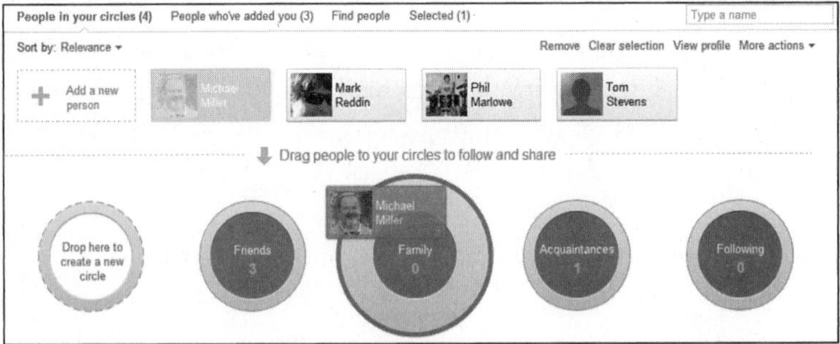

Figure 7.3: *Dragging and dropping a friend into a circle.*

Remember, you can add a single person to multiple circles. Just drag and drop that person onto a different circle.

Managing Your Circles

The makeup of your circles doesn't have to remain constant over time. You can add new people to existing circles, of course; you can also delete people from certain circles or even delete entire circles.

Viewing Friends in Circles

Can't remember who is in a given circle? Then it's time to open that circle and peek inside.

First, you can view thumbnail pictures of a circle's inhabitants by merely hovering over that circle on the circles page. As you can see in Figure 7.4, this gives you a good visual overview of who's in that circle.

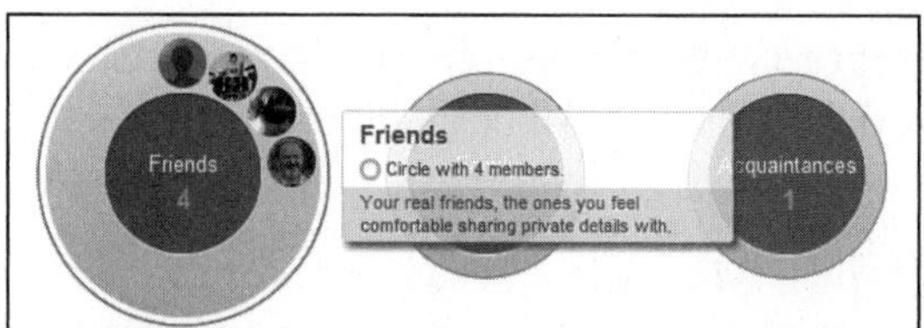

Figure 7.4: *Quick viewing members of a circle.*

Next, you can click the circle. This displays the dialog box shown in Figure 7.5, with circle members listed.

Figure 7.5: *Viewing all members of a circle.*

If you'd rather see a full page devoted to the members of a circle, just click the circle on the circles page. This adds a tab for this circle to the tab list at the top of the circles page, as shown in Figure 7.6, with all circle members displayed there.

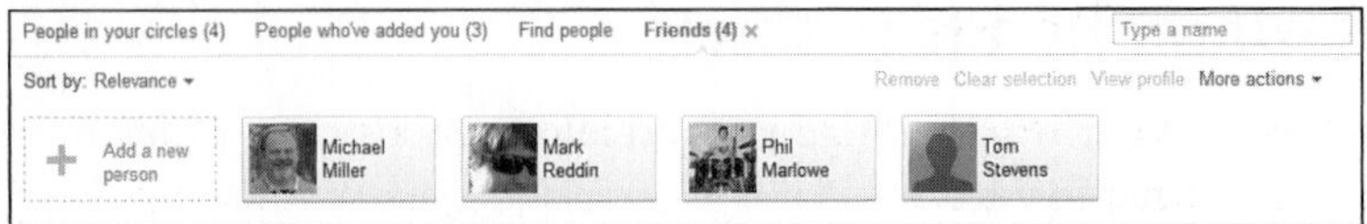

Figure 7.6: *Members of a circle displayed in a new tab.*

Deleting Friends from Circles

To keep your circles relevant, you'll want to trim the ranks from time to time, deleting those friends you no longer want to communicate with. Here's how to remove friends from a given circle:

1. From the circles page, click the circle you want to edit.
2. When the dialog box for that circle appears, click those friends you want to remove, as shown in Figure 7.7. You can select multiple people at the same time.

Figure 7.7: *Deleting people from a circle.*

3. Click the **Remove** link.
4. Click the **Save** button.

The folks you selected will be removed from this circle. You can, however, add them back to the circle at a later time, if you like.

Deleting Circles

Sometimes you find that a given circle no longer makes sense for you. Perhaps you created a circle for a project that has since ended; perhaps you just have a circle that you never added anyone to. Fortunately, Google+ lets you easily delete circles—and all the people included in them.

To delete a circle and its members, follow these steps:

1. From the circles page, right-click the circle you want to delete.
2. Select **Delete Circle** from the pop-up menu.
3. When the Delete Your Circle dialog box appears, click the **Delete Circle** button.

GOOGLE+ INSIDER

Customization is the name of the game with circles. Just as you can create any type of circle, you can likewise delete any circle, including Google+'s four default circles.

Posting to Circles

I'll talk more about posting to Google+ in Chapter 9. For now, know that when you create a Google+ post, you can select who it's sent to by using circles.

When you create a post, you have the following sending options:

Specific circles. You choose which of your circles will receive the post. You can select one circle or multiple circles; the members of those circles will see your post.

Your Circles. The post is sent to anyone who is in any of your circles.

Extended Circles. The post is sent to all the members of your circles, as well as all the members of their circles. Think of this as an "extended family" metaphor; your post gets sent to both your friends and friends of your friends.

Public. The post is sent to anyone who has added you to one of their circles, even if they're not currently in any of yours. Public posts are also visible to anyone viewing your Google+ Profile.

Specific contacts. You can also indicate specific individuals to receive your post.

As you can see, the easiest route is to specify specific circles when making a post. You can then send one kind of post to one circle and another kind of post to another circle. Members of your other circles will never know that you made the post; it's a great way to segment your Google+ posting.

GOOGLE+ PLUS

Circles solves the perennial social networking issue of how to post to your friends without your boss, parents, or teachers seeing it. Put all your casual friends into a Friends circle, and make sure your boss, parents, or teachers are not in that circle. Then create a post and send it only to your Friends circle; all those other folks won't receive the post, and you're safe.

Reading Posts from Your Circles

Likewise, you can choose to filter your Google+ Stream to view only posts from people in selected circles. I'll cover this in more depth in Chapter 8, but suffice to say it's as easy as clicking the name of a circle on the streams page. This displays a stream consisting solely of posts from the selected circle. It makes it a whole lot easier to read only those posts you're interested in at the moment.

The Least You Need to Know

- Google+ is built around the concept of circles of friends.
- Google+ lets you organize your friends into different circles.
- You can then direct your posts to members of specific circles.
- You can also filter your stream to read only posts from members of a given circle.

Reading the Stream

Chapter **8**

In This Chapter

- Filtering your stream's contents
- Removing unwanted posts and blocking unwanted users
- Commenting on posts in the stream
- How to +1 the posts you like
- Sharing your favorite posts

To keep abreast of what your friends are up to, you need to read the posts they make to Google+. You do this via something called the stream—literally, a stream of posts from all your Google+ friends.

That sounds easy enough. But did you know you can customize your stream to show only posts from selected circles? Or that you can block unwanted posts? Or comment on posts that interest you? Or even share posts you like with others?

That's right, there's a lot you can do with the contents of your Google+ Stream. Read on to learn how to customize the stream, block unwanted posts, comment on posts, share posts with others, and more.

Understanding the Stream

The stream is what you see when you go to your Google+ home page. In fact, for most of us, the stream will be the go-to page on Google+. It's the one page you visit to keep informed about what all your friends are doing.

As its name implies, the stream is a constant stream or feed of all the posts made by all your friends on Google+. Whatever your friends post shows up in the stream, and the newest posts are at the top.

GOOGLE+ INSIDER

The Google+ Stream serves a similar function as Facebook's News Feed or the Twitter Feed, in that it consolidates posts from all the people you follow. The major difference is the way the circles help you filter what appears in the stream.

In this fashion, the stream centralizes all the content that people in your circles have opted to share with you. This includes the standard text posts, of course, but also links to interesting web pages, pictures, videos, and even location markers that tell you where your friends are or have been. The stream contains everything you need or care about, all in one place.

That said, you don't have to view everything in the stream all at once. Because of Google+'s circles functionality, you can filter the stream to display only posts from a selected circle. It's a great way to keep track of only those people you're interested in at the moment. If you need a little refresher on using your circles, revisit Chapter 7.

Viewing Posts in the Stream

Reading your stream isn't that hard, although there are some tricks involved. And it always helps to know just what it is you're reading.

The first thing you need to know is exactly where the stream is located; after all, there's no stream button in Google+'s set of navigation buttons. Instead, the stream is a part of your Google+'s home page, so click the **Home** button to go there and view your stream.

As you can see in Figure 8.1, the stream inhabits the big middle column of the home page. The smaller column on the left contains navigational elements, as well as the means to filter your stream by circle. The column on the right is more informational, and includes suggestions on people to add to your circles. So the middle column is where it's at.

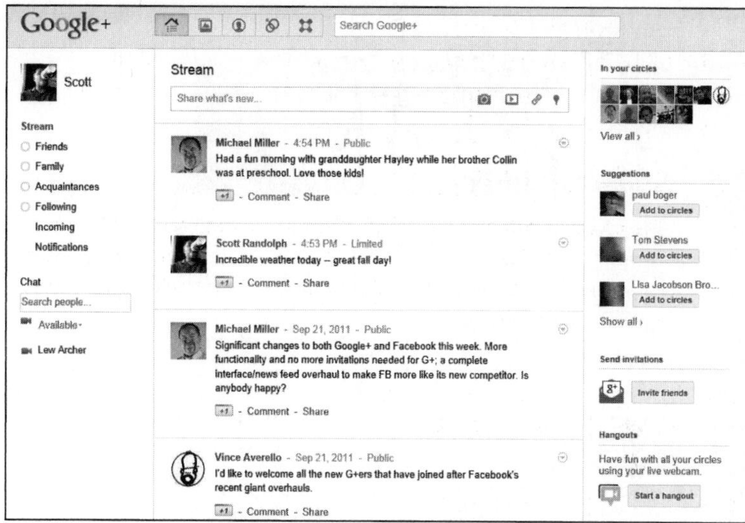

Figure 8.1: *Viewing the stream on your Google+ home page.*

Within the stream you see a series of posts made by all the people in your circles. These posts are displayed in reverse chronological order—meaning that the most recent posts are at the top and the older ones are at the bottom. To view even older updates, scroll to the bottom of the page and click the **More** link.

Most of the posts you find in your stream are short text messages, such as the one in Figure 8.2, although posts can also include photos, videos, location notices, and links to other web pages.

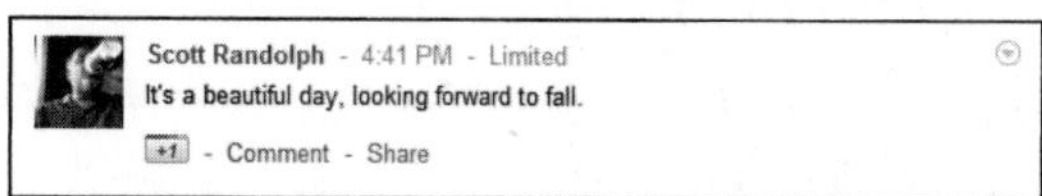

Figure 8.2: *A standard text post in the stream.*

If there's a photo in a post, like the one shown in Figure 8.3, click the photo to view it at a larger size on a new page. Click the **X** on this page or press the **Esc** key to return to your stream.

Figure 8.3: *A post with photos attached.*

If there's a video in the status update, like the one shown in Figure 8.4, simply click the video to begin playback on a new page. The video player on the new page includes the standard Pause/Play control, along with a Mute/Volume control and a Full Screen button, all found directly beneath the video window. Click the **X** on the top of this page or press the **Esc** key to return to your stream.

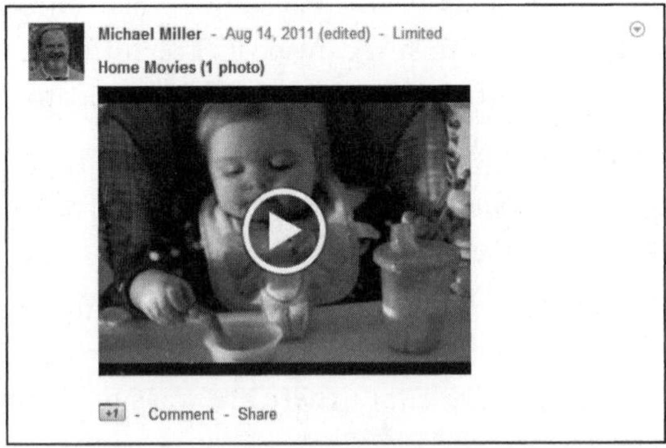

Figure 8.4: *A post with a video attached.*

If there's a link in the post, such as the one shown in Figure 8.5, click it to leave Google+ and open the linked-to page in a new browser tab. Pretty straightforward, really.

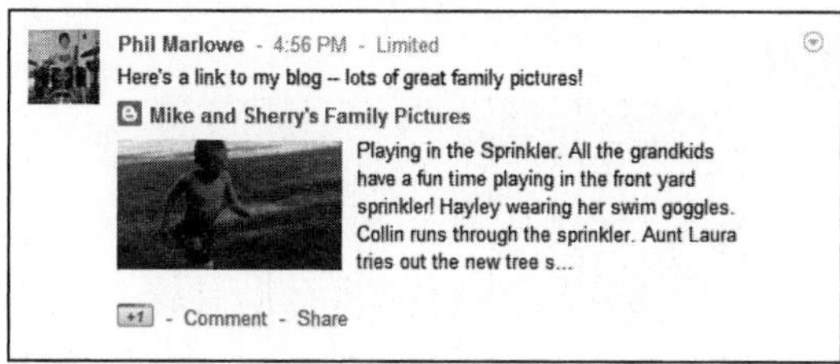

Figure 8.5: *A post with a link to another web page.*

If other people have commented on a post, those comments are displayed beneath the post, as shown in Figure 8.6. There's more to come in a moment about how to leave your own comments on a post.

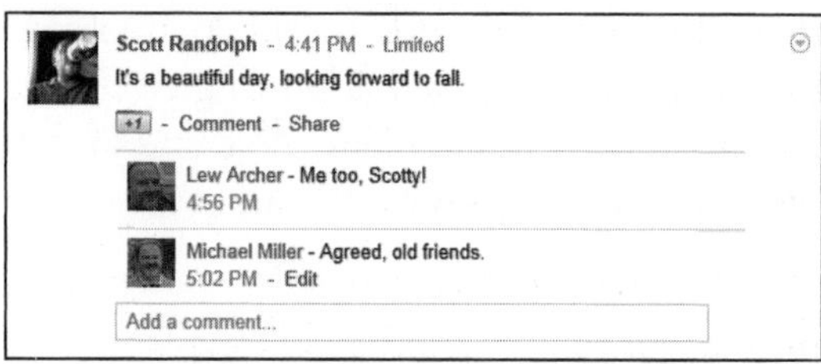

Figure 8.6: *A post with comments.*

Customizing the Stream

By default, all the posts from all the friends in all your circles appear in your stream. That's fine, but if you have a lot of friends, it can get a little overwhelming. Fortunately, there are ways to customize and filter the content of your stream.

Viewing a Stream for a Specific Circle

The easiest way to filter your stream's content is to display content only from a specific circle. You select what content you want displayed in your stream by making a selection from the left-hand navigation column, as shown in Figure 8.7. Just click an option and your stream changes to display only the selected content.

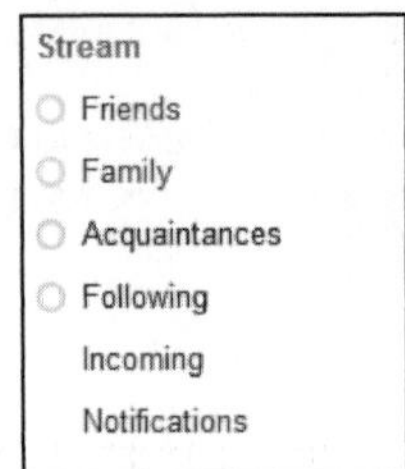

Figure 8.7: *Filtering the content of your stream by circle.*

Here are the viewing options available:

Stream. Click the **Stream** link to view all the posts from all your friends in your stream. This is the "full stream" option.

Specific circles. All your circles are listed here, including the default Friends, Family, Acquaintances, and Following circles, as well as any custom circles you've created. Click the name of a circle to only display posts from that circle in the stream.

Incoming. This displays posts from people who have you in their circles, but who are not in your circles. These posts might be interesting (but probably not that interesting, or you'd have added these folks to your circles already). Still, it's potentially fun to know what people who are interested in you are posting.

Notifications. This displays notices and messages from Google+, including notice of people who've added you to their circles or commented on your posts.

Like I said, filtering your stream is as easy as clicking one of these options in the left column. Click another option to change the filter.

Removing (Muting) a Post

Sometimes somebody posts something that you just don't care to read, and don't want clogging up your feed. Or, you might have made a post that you've decided to kill. Fortunately, Google+ lets you remove (in their terminology, "mute") any single post. Muting a post makes it go away.

GOOGLE+ INSIDER

Muting a post removes only the selected post and any related comments. It does not remove other posts by that person.

To remove a post, follow these steps:

1. Navigate to the offending post in your stream.
2. Click the down-arrow on the top right of the post, as shown in Figure 8.8.
3. Select **Mute This Post** from the pop-up menu.

That's it; the post is now removed.

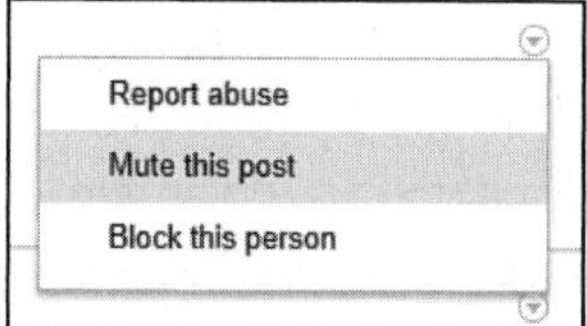

Figure 8.8: *Removing a post.*

Blocking Unwanted Posters

What do you do if a particular person consistently posts messages that are offensive or insulting? Google+ lets you block individual posters, so you don't see anything they post in the future.

Follow these steps to block an individual:

1. Go to a post by that person and click on their name.
2. This opens that person's profile page. Scroll to the bottom of the left column and click **Block** ***Name***.
3. When the confirmation dialog box appears, click the **Block** ***Name*** button.

When you block someone, you'll no longer see that person's posts in your stream, even in the incoming stream. The blocked individual will be removed from any circles of yours they were in, and they also won't appear in any of your extended circles (circles of your friends). They won't be able to view any new content you post, although your existing posts won't disappear from their stream. However, they won't be able to comment on them

Responding to Posts

Google+ is a social network, which means it's all about encouraging social interaction amongst its users. To that end, you can comment on your friends' posts, share those posts with others, and even "like" a post.

+1'ing a Post

Let's start with the "liking" thing. When you find a post you find particularly appealing, but don't want to spend the time commenting on it, you can indicate that you liked the post. You do this by clicking the **+1** button beneath the post, as shown in Figure 8.9.

Figure 8.9: *Google's +1 button.*

Google's +1 option is used to indicate that you like, agree with, or recommend specific content. You find the +1 button all over the web, including in Google's web search results.

Commenting on a Post

When you want to engage a friend on a given topic, the easiest way to do so is to comment on their post. All comments appear beneath the post in a type of message thread.

To comment on a post, follow these steps:

1. Navigate to the post in your stream.
2. Click the **Comment** link beneath the post.

3. This opens a new comments box beneath the post, as shown in Figure 8.10. Enter your comments into the text box.

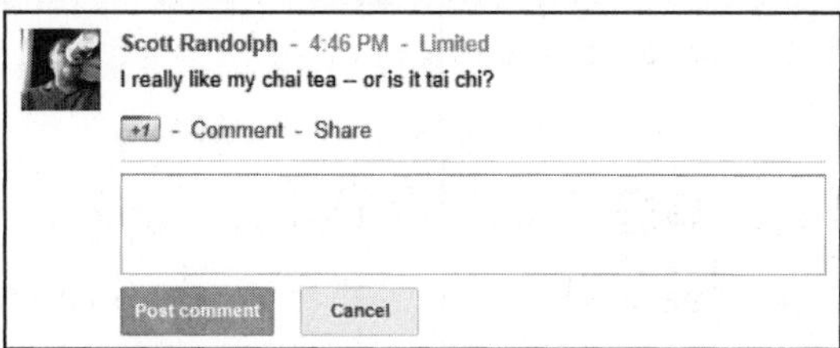

Figure 8.10: *Commenting on a post.*

4. Click the **Post Comment** button when done.

Your comment now appears beneath the original post. Others can add their own comments to the original post, or comment on your comment. In addition, the original poster can reply to your comments, as he or she wishes.

Sharing a Post

If you really like a post, you may want to share it with other friends or circles on Google+. This is easy enough to do, and is a great way to pass around the content that you like.

To share a post, follow these steps:

1. Navigate to the post in your stream.
2. Click the **Share** link beneath the post.
3. If prompted to be thoughtful with whom you share, click the **Okay, Got It!** button.
4. Google+ now opens a new Share This Post dialog box. Enter your comments on this post into the top text box.
5. Go to the bottom text box and enter or select the names of circles or individuals with whom you'd like to share the post.
6. Click the **Share** button.

Linking to a Post

You can also share posts outside of Google+, by including a link to the post in an email, blog post, or whatever. To link to a post in this fashion, follow these steps:

1. Navigate to the desired post in your stream.
2. Click the down-arrow on the top right of the post and select **Link to This Post**.
3. The post now opens in its own browser tab. Copy the URL from this tab's address box.
4. Paste the URL into your email or blog post.

Anyone clicking the link you just pasted will go to a dedicated web page for the post you liked.

The Least You Need to Know

- The stream, located on your Google+ home page, displays all the posts made by all the people in your Google+ Circles.
- You can filter the stream to display only posts from selected circles.
- Posts can be simple text messages or contain web links, photos, videos, and the like.
- You can comment on any given post, or just "like" the post by using Google's +1 feature.
- You can also share posts, either with fellow Google+ users, members of circles, or people not using Google+.

Posting to the Stream

Chapter 9

In This Chapter

- Posting only to specific circles or individuals
- Posting links to web pages, photos, videos, and your location
- Posting from the Google navigation bar
- Mentioning friends in your posts

So far in this book I've talked a lot about viewing posts from your friends and circles. But your friends also want to read what you're up to, which means you need to make a few posts of your own. How do you post to Google+? And what can you include in a post? Those are the posting basics covered in this chapter.

What Is a Post?

A post on Google+ is how you update your friends on what you're doing. It's a short snapshot into your life at this moment, as posted to the Google+ site.

The posts you make appear in multiple places on the Google+ site. First, your posts appear on your own profile page, on your Posts tab. More important, your posts also appear on the stream section of your friends' home pages. This way your friends are kept updated as to what you're doing and thinking.

At its most basic, a Google+ post is a brief text message. It can be as short as a word or two, or it can be several paragraphs long; that's up to you.

GOOGLE+ INSIDER

Unlike Twitter, which has a 140-character limit on its tweets, Google has no real limit on how long your posts can be.

Although a basic post is all text, you can also attach various items to your posts, including digital photographs, videos, and links to other web pages. You can also "tag" other Google+ users in your posts, so that their names appear as clickable links (to their profile pages, of course).

The convenient thing about posting on Google+ is that it's a post-once, read-many process. That is, a single post is broadcast to multiple people in the circles you specify. If a circle has a dozen members, that's a dozen people who can read the message you posted.

And, as I just mentioned, you can specify exactly whom you want to view each post you make. You do this by selecting one or more groups while you're making the post. The post is then sent only to members of those specific groups. It's a great way to separate the different things you may post about.

Creating a New Post

When you want your friends on Google+ to know what you're up to or thinking, you need to post about it. When you create a post, you can choose who can view it—typically by selecting one or more circles. Only those people or circles you select will see your post in their streams; this way you can send specific posts to specific people only.

Posting to Google+

How do you make a post? It's quite easy. Just follow these steps:

1. Go to your Google+ home page.
2. At the top of the Stream section is a Share What's New box, like the one shown in Figure 9.1. Enter your message into this box.

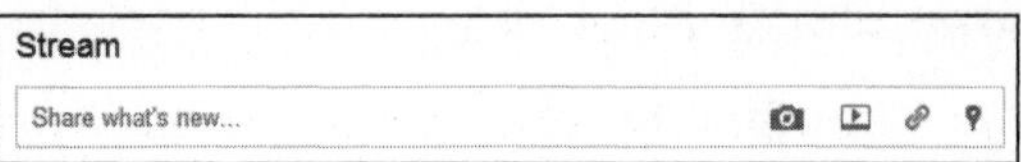

Figure 9.1: *Getting ready to make a post.*

3. As you type your message, the Share box expands, as shown in Figure 9.2. If this is the first post you've made, click the **Add Circles or People to Share With** link.

Figure 9.2: *Creating your first post.*

4. If you've previously posted, the last circles you posted to will be displayed, as shown in Figure 9.3. You can accept these circles, or click the **X** next to any circle to remove it from this post. To add other circles, click the **Add More People** link.

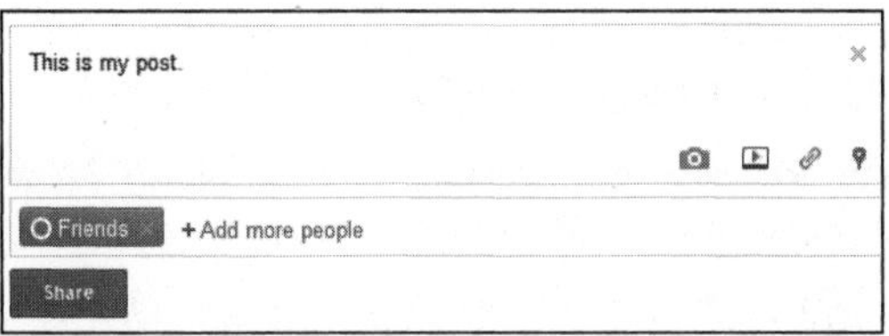

Figure 9.3: *Creating a new post; the circles selected for your last post are already listed.*

5. From the pop-up menu shown in Figure 9.4, select those specific circles you want to view your post. You can also choose to send this post to people in all your circles (All Circles), people in your friends' circles (Extended Circles), or to anyone who has added you to their circles (Public).

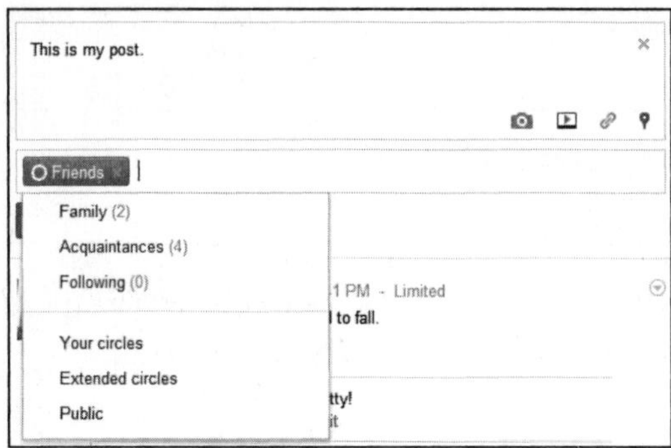

Figure 9.4: *Selecting who can view your new post.*

6. When you're done creating the post, click the **Share** button.

Your post will now be visible in the streams of those people you selected.

Sending a Private Post

You can also use Google+ to send private posts to individual users. These posts will appear in the recipient's stream, but not in the streams of any other users.

Here's how to do it:

1. Go to your Google+ home page.
2. Enter your message into the Share What's New box at the top of the page.
3. Click the **X** to close any circles previously selected beneath the Share box.
4. Click the **Add Circles or People to Share With** link and enter the person's name or email address.
5. The person's name now appears beneath your post, as shown in Figure 9.5. Click the **Share** button to send the post.

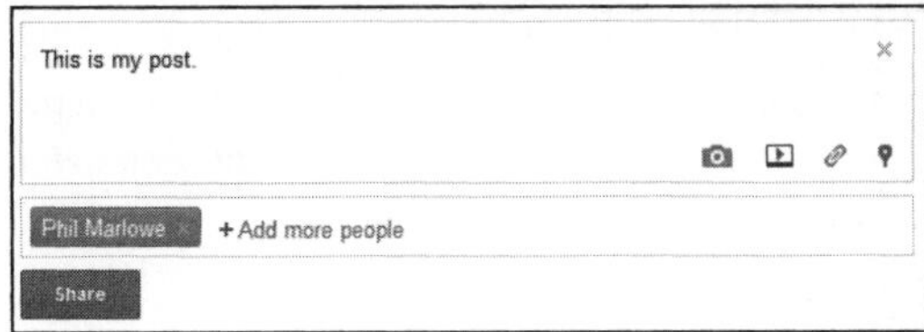

Figure 9.5: *Sending a private post to a single recipient.*

Formatting Your Post

Now for some fun stuff. Most posts are text-only posts. But you can format the text in your post—if you know the secret formatting codes. There's no formatting toolbar, you see; you have to enter the codes manually.

What kind of formatting can you do? Table 9.1 provides the details:

Table 9.1: Google+ Post Formatting

Formatting	Example	Code
Bold	**Word**	*Word*
Italic	*Word*	_Word_
Strikethrough	~~Word~~	-Word-

So, for example, you want to bold a word in your post, you put an asterisk (*) before and after the word. If you want to italicize a sentence, put an underline mark (_) before the first word in the sentence and another after the last. It's not much, but it can spice up your posts.

Attaching Items to a Post

You can also add other content to your posts, in the form of links to web pages, digital photos, videos, and location markers. You add these items when you're first creating your post.

GOOGLE+ PLUS

You can also add items to a post by dragging those items and dropping them onto the share box, or by cutting and pasting them.

Sharing Web Links

If you find a web page you think your friends may be interested in, you can share a link to that page in a post. Here's how to do it:

1. Go to your Google+ home page and enter your (optional) text message into the Share What's New box.
2. Click the **Add** Link (chain) icon.
3. This expands the Share box to include a Type or Paste a Link box, as shown in Figure 9.6. As the box suggests, type or paste the URL of the page you want to link to into this box, then click the **Add** button.

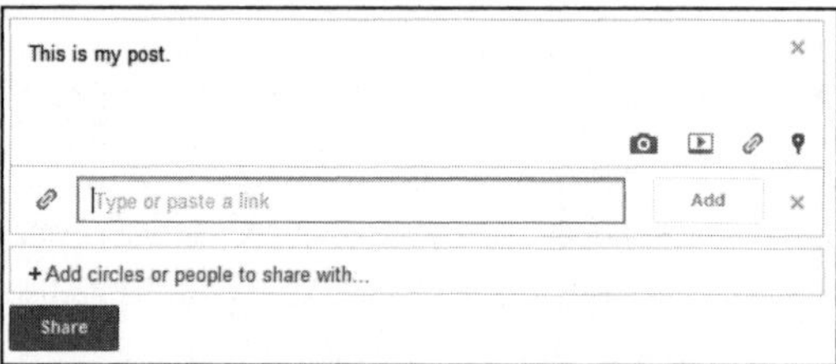

Figure 9.6: *Getting ready to add a link to a post.*

4. Google+ now displays the name of the website, along with brief descriptive text and, in many cases, a thumbnail image from the site (as shown in Figure 9.7). If there are multiple images to choose from, the thumbnail includes right and left arrows; click these arrows to select an image to display, or click the **X** on the thumbnail to not display an image in your post.

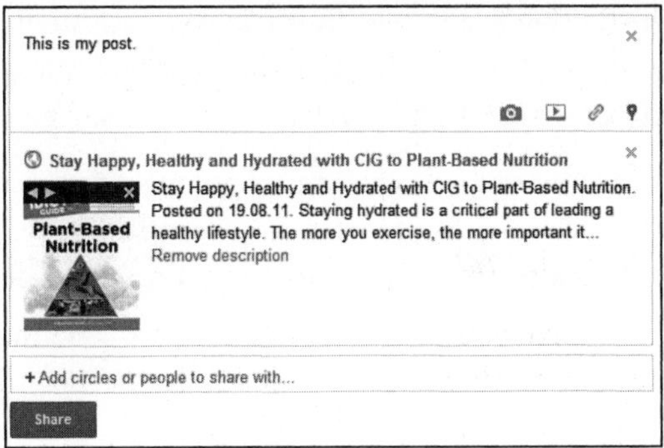

Figure 9.7: *Viewing the web page's description and thumbnail image.*

5. If you'd rather not display the site description in your post, click the **Remove Description** link.
6. Select which circles or individuals will view your post.
7. Click the **Share** button.

Sharing Photos

There are actually two ways to share photos via a Google+ post: you can upload photos from your computer or upload photos from your mobile phone. I'll explain the PC-based method here, and save the mobile uploading for Chapter 15.

GOOGLE+ INSIDER

You also have the option of uploading photos to a photo album, which can then be shared with your friends. Learn more in Chapter 12.

To share a picture from your computer, then, follow these steps:

1. Go to your Google+ home page and enter your (optional) text message into the Share What's New box.
2. Click the **Add Photos** (camera) icon.
3. Select **Add Photos** from the pop-up menu.

4. When the Open window appears, navigate to and select the photos you want to add. (You can include multiple photos in a single post.)

5. Google+ now uploads the photo(s) you selected, then displays them beneath the Share box, as shown in Figure 9.8. To add more photos to this post, click the **Add More** link.

Figure 9.8: *A photo added to a post.*

6. To edit a photo you've attached, click the **Edit Photos** link. This displays the Edit Photos panel, shown in Figure 9.9. Hover over a photo to rotate the photo, delete the photo, or add a caption to the photo. Click the **Done** button when you're done editing.

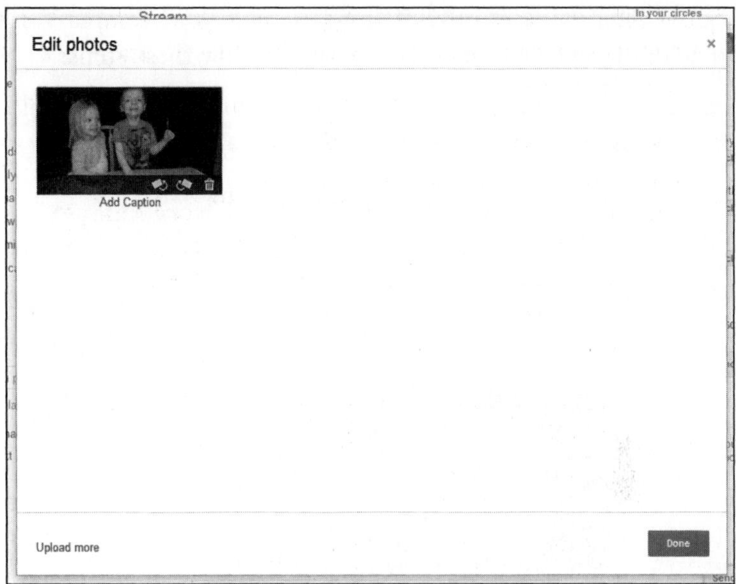

Figure 9.9: *Editing a photo attached to a post.*

7. Back on your stream page, select which circles or individuals will view your post.
8. Click the **Share** button when you're ready to post the post.

GOOGLE+ INSIDER

Google+ accepts photos in most common image formats such as GIF, PNG, and JPEG. Each can be up to 2048 × 2048 pixels in size. Photos larger than this will be automatically resized when uploaded.

Sharing Videos

Just as you can attach digital photos to your Google+ posts, you can also attach home movies, in the form of digital videos. You can share videos stored on your computer or videos you like on the YouTube site. (You can also upload videos from your mobile phone, but that's a topic for Chapter 15.)

First up is the process of uploading videos from your computer. It's not much different than uploading photos; follow these steps:

1. Go to your Google+ home page and enter your (optional) text message into the Share What's New box.
2. Click the **Add Video** (play button) icon.
3. Select **Upload Video** from the pop-up menu.
4. When the Upload Videos panel appears, as shown in Figure 9.10, click the **Select Videos from Your Computer** button.

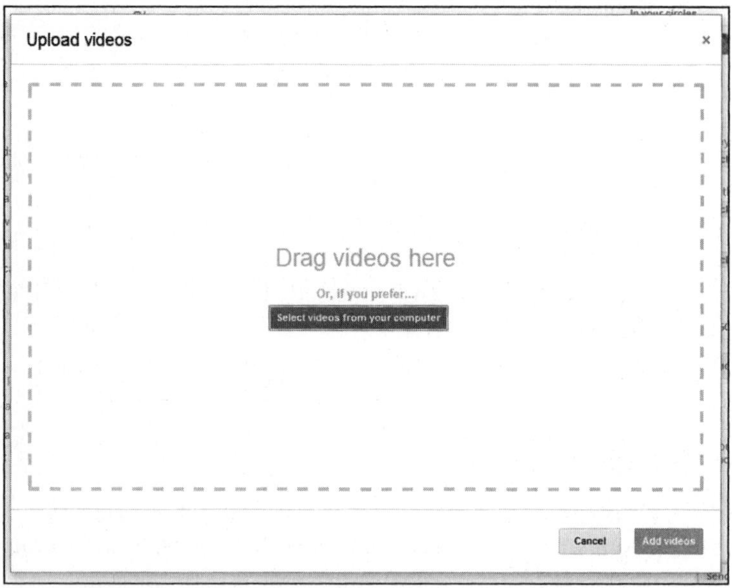

Figure 9.10: *Getting ready to add a video to a post.*

5. When the Open window appears, navigate to and select the video you want to add.
6. Google+ now uploads the video you selected, then displays that video in the Upload Videos panel. Click the **Add Videos** button to add this video to your post.
7. The video now appears beneath the Share box on your stream page, as shown in Figure 9.11. Select which circles or individuals will view your post.

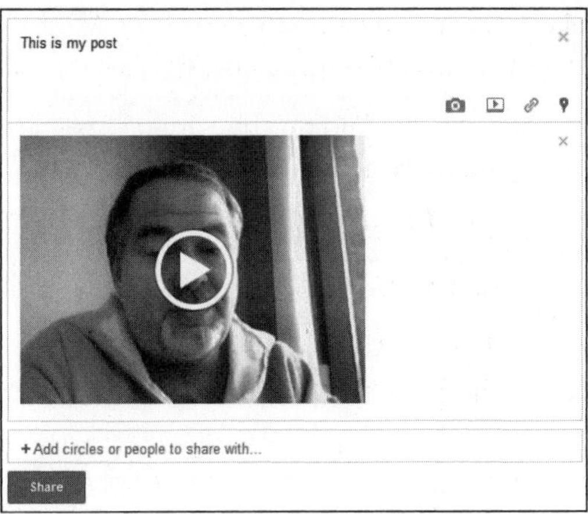

Figure 9.11: *A video added to a post in progress.*

8. Click the **Share** button when you're ready to post the post.

GOOGLE+ INSIDER

Google+ accepts videos in most common video formats and resolutions, all the way up to 1080p resolution. You can upload videos up to 15 minutes in length.

Sharing a YouTube Video

Google+ also lets you post videos that you find on its sister site, YouTube. You can do this from the YouTube site itself or from your Google+ home page. I'll examine the latter option here; follow these steps:

1. Go to your Google+ home page and enter your (optional) text message into the Share What's New box.
2. Click the **Add Video** (play button) icon.
3. Select **YouTube** from the pop-up menu.
4. You now see the Choose a YouTube video panel, shown in Figure 9.12. To select one of your own videos, select the **Your YouTube Videos** tab. Alternatively, you can search for any video by selecting the **Search** tab, entering your query, and clicking the **Search** (magnifying glass) button.

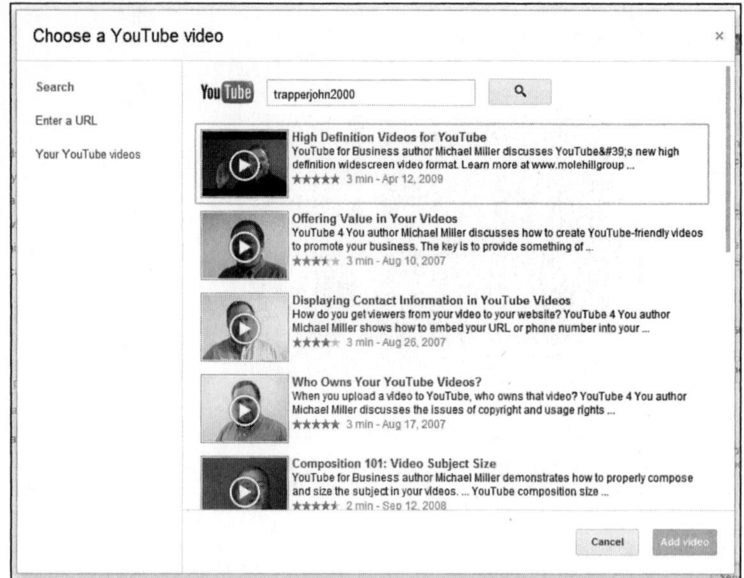

Figure 9.12: *Selecting a YouTube video to post.*

5. Click the video you want to include, then click the **Add Video** button.

6. The chosen video now appears beneath the Share box on your Stream page, as shown in Figure 9.13. Select which circles or individuals will view your post.

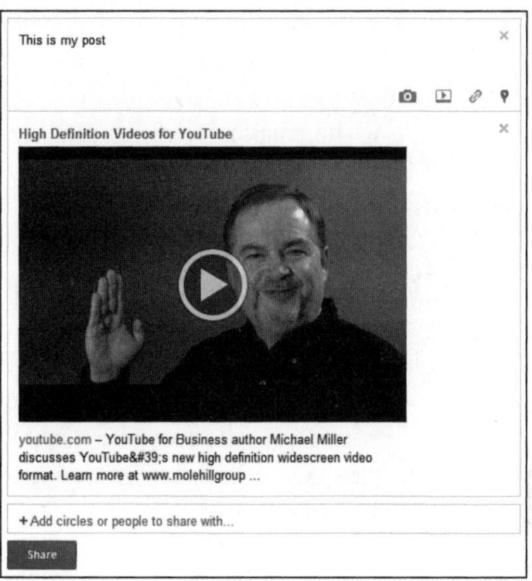

Figure 9.13: *A YouTube video added to a post in progress.*

7. Click the **Share** button when you're ready to post the post.

Sharing Your Location

Google+ lets you include your current location in any post. This is nice if you want your friends to know where you are at the moment. Follow these steps to add this information to a post:

GOOGLE+ MINUS

Be careful about including your location in your posts. This can let robbers know that you're not at home, or let stalkers know where to find you.

1. Go to your Google+ home page and enter your (optional) text message into the Share What's New box.
2. Click the **Add Your Location** (pinpoint) icon.

3. The first time you use this feature, your web browser may prompt you to let Google+ track your location. (Figure 9.14 shows a typical message to this affect.) If you want your location tracked, allow the tracking at this point.

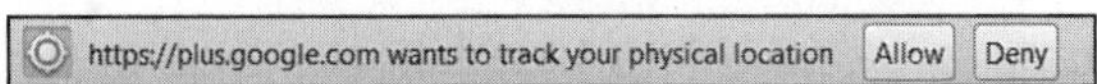

Figure 9.14: *Look for the browser prompt to allow location tracking.*

4. Google+ will now attempt to determine your location. If it can, it displays your location under the Share box, as shown in Figure 9.15. If it can't, it tells you. (It's also possible, of course, that Google+ gets your location wrong—which means you may need to edit it.)

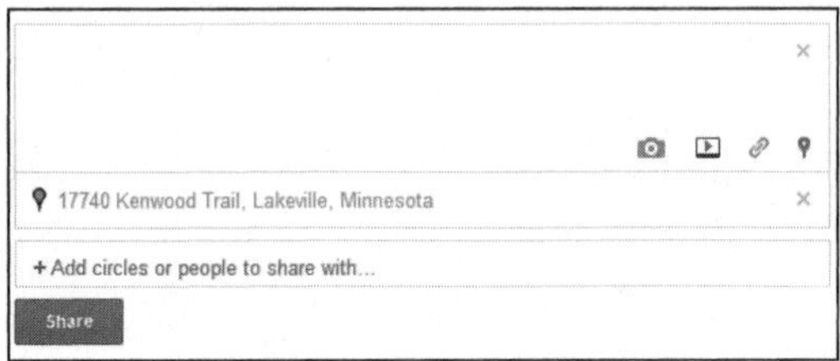

Figure 9.15: *Your location added to a post.*

5. Select which circles or individuals will view your post.
6. Click the **Share** button when you're ready to post the post.

Mentioning Others in Your Posts

Here's something interesting about Google+ posts. You can mention other users in your posts, which makes their names in the posts clickable. This helps other friends link through to the friends you mention.

To do this, all you have to do is enter the @ character, followed by the person's name. In fact, as you start to type the name, Google+ will display a list of matching contacts, a shown in Figure 9.16; select your friend from this list, or finish entering the name manually.

Figure 9.16: *Mentioning a friend's name in a post.*

When you make the post, the person's name appears as a clickable blue link in the post. Clicking the name opens that person's Google+ profile page.

Posting from the Google Navigation Bar

You don't have to limit your Google+ posts to when you're on the Google+ site. You can also post from your mobile phone (discussed in Chapter 15) or from just about any Google site or service, by using the Google navigation bar.

All you have to do is visit a Google site, such as Google web search (www.google.com) or Gmail (www.gmail.com) that displays the Google navigation bar, shown in Figure 9.17, then follow these steps:

Figure 9.17: *The Google navigation bar, found on most Google sites.*

1. Click the **Share** box in the navigation bar.
2. This opens the Share pane, shown in Figure 9.18. Enter your post as you would normally; you can also attach photos, videos, links, and location information, if you wish.

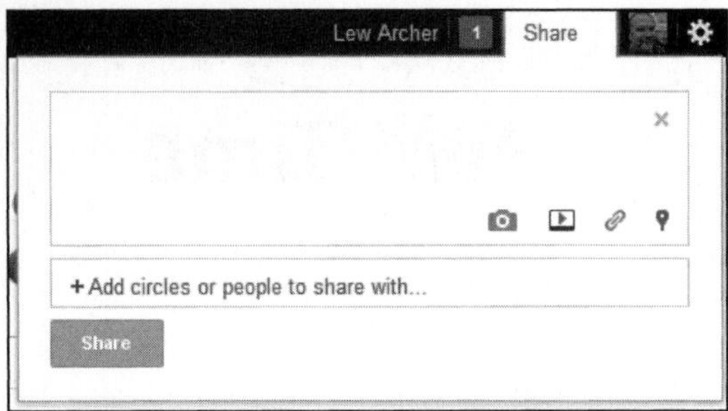

Figure 9.18: *Making a post from the Google navigation bar.*

3. Select which circles or individuals will view your post.
4. Click the **Share** button when you're ready to post the post.

The Least You Need to Know

- You keep your friends up to date on what you're doing by making posts to Google+.
- Your posts appear in your friends' stream, and on your profile page.
- You can direct your posts only to specific circles or individuals.
- Your posts can include links to web pages, photos, videos, and information about your location.
- Posts can also include clickable links to friends you mention in the post.
- You can post from the Google+ home page or from the Google navigation bar.

Chapter 10

Chatting in Real Time

In This Chapter

- How Google+ chat works
- Initiating a text chat
- Inviting others for a group chat
- Starting a voice chat

In the previous chapter I explained how to post public messages on Google+. While this is an efficient means of communication, it isn't necessarily the fastest way to communicate, especially if your friends don't monitor their Google+ streams 24/7.

If you want a more immediate means of communicating with friends, family, and co-workers, check out Google+'s chat feature. This lets you communicate in real time with your friends, using one-to-one text messages. Unlike regular posts, these are totally private communications; no one but you and the person you're talking to can read them.

Understanding Google+ Chat

In Google+ parlace, "chat" means *instant messaging*. You're probably familiar with how instant messaging (IM) works; Google+ chat is essentially an IM service built into the Google+ network. It's based on the Google Talk IM service, so you can chat with other people who use either Google+ or Google Talk.

DEFINITION

Instant messaging is a type of real-time, text-based communication between two or more computer users. It's very similar to texting with a mobile phone, but takes place on your computer.

There are several different IM services available, the most popular of which are Google Talk, Yahoo! Messenger, AOL Instant Messenger (AIM), ICQWindows Live Messenger, and Skype. In general, these IM services don't talk to each other; you can only chat with other people who use the same service you do.

Google+ Chat works just like these more traditional IM services, but is exclusive to Google users. Not just Google+ users, by the way; it works with anyone using any form of the Google Talk IM service.

As such, Google+ Chat lets you carry on real-time conversations with any of your Google+ friends who are also logged on to the site. Obviously, you can't talk with someone who isn't logged on. But as long as a friend is online in Google+ at the same time you are, you can chat to your heart's delight.

Chatting, by the way, consists of sending and receiving sequential text messages to and from your friend. Basic chat is text-based; Google+ also offers voice and video chat, if you and your friends have the proper equipment installed on your computers.

You're not limited to conducting one chat session at a time, by the way. Google+ lets you open multiple chat windows simultaneously, so you can conduct more than one one-on-one chat—separate chats with separate people. And you're not limited to chatting one-on-one, as Google+ lets you chat with multiple friends in a group chat. This is great if you're collaborating on a business project with people in different locations, and need to conduct a group meeting; just launch a group chat of some sort and get the project moving.

And remember, Google+ offers more than just simple text chat. You can also participate in voice chats, which are like internet phone calls, and video chats, where you can actually see who you're talking to (learn more about video chatting in Chapter 11). Use whichever type of chat makes sense for you and your friends.

GOOGLE+ INSIDER

For text chat, all you need is a computer or mobile phone. For audio chat, you'll need to have a microphone and speakers (or a USB headset) attached to your computer.

Conducting Text Chats

We'll start by examining Google+ text chat, which is the most popular type of chat—probably because it's the easiest to do.

Google+'s chat feature is accessed from your Google+ home page, at the bottom of the left column. As you can see in Figure 10.1, the Chat section displays those friends on your chat list. Next to each name is an icon of some sort. If the icon is round, the person is available for text chat only; if it's a video camera icon, the person is available for video chat, too.

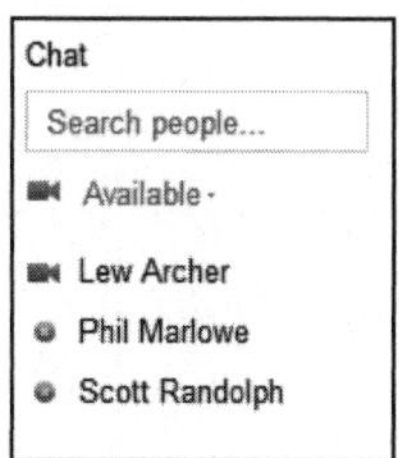

Figure 10.1: *The Chat section on a Google+ home page.*

These icons are of different colors that reflect the person's availability to chat. Table 10.1 details what each color icon means.

Table 10.1: Google+ Chat Status Icons

Color	Status
Green	Online and available to chat
Yellow	Online but idle
Red	Online but busy
Gray	Offline

Inviting Others to Join Your Chat List

By default, the chat list displays people you've already chosen to talk with in either Google+ or Google Talk. To display (and chat with) other friends, you have to invite them to chat with you—which you do from the search box in the Chat section.

To invite someone into your chat list, follow these steps:

1. Go to the Google+ home page.
2. In the Chat section, type the person's name or email box into the search box.
3. When the menu option appears, as shown in Figure 10.2, click **Invite to Chat**.

Figure 10.2: *Inviting a new friend to chat.*

4. Google+ prompts you that this person will need to accept your invitation before you can chat. Click the **Send Invite** button.

The person now receives an invitation to join your chat list, like the one shown in Figure 10.3. If you receive such an invitation, you can accept by clicking the **Yes** button—or decline by clicking **No**.

Figure 10.3: *Viewing an invitation to chat.*

Starting a Chat

To chat with a friend, that person must be online and available—indicated by a green icon next to his or her name in the chat list. You can then start the chat by following these steps:

1. Click that person's name in your chat list.
2. This opens a new chat window at the bottom right of the Google+ screen, like the one shown in Figure 10.4. Enter a message in the bottom text box, and then press **Enter**.

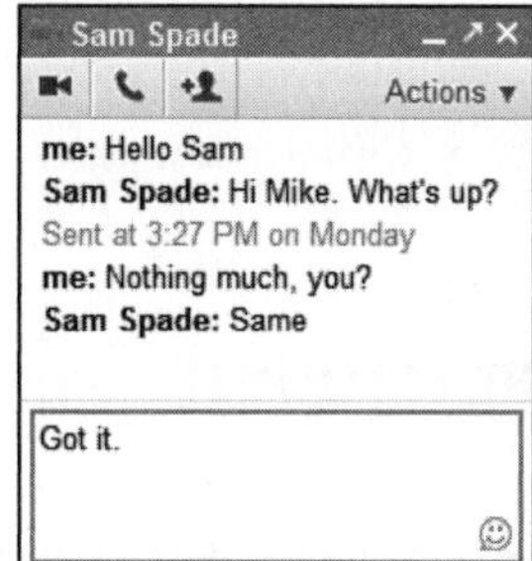

Figure 10.4: *Chatting with a friend.*

Your message is now displayed in the main window, and sent to your friend. When your friend replies, his message is also displayed in the main window. To end a chat session, simply close the chat window.

By the way, you can display your chat session in a separate window, instead of within the Google+ page. Just click the **Pop-Out** (diagonal arrow) button to open a separate chat window. Click the **Pop-In** button to return to the normal chat window.

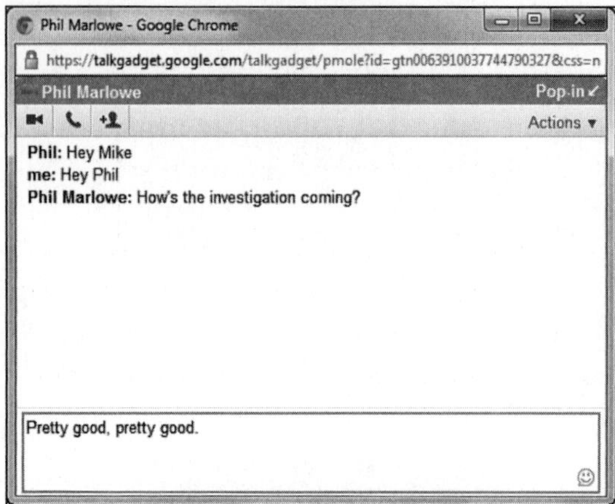

Figure 10.5: *Chatting in a pop-out window.*

Answering a Chat Request

When someone wants to chat with you, you see a chat window pop up at the bottom of your Google+ screen. To respond and start chatting, simply type a reply into the bottom text box, and press **Enter**. To ignore the chat, just close the window.

Sending a File via Chat

Google+ lets you send files to the people you're chatting with. It's a quick and easy way to exchange pictures and other files in real time. Here's how to do it:

1. From within the chat window, click the **Actions** button.
2. Select **Send a File**.
3. When the Open or Choose File window appears, navigate to and select the files to send, then click **Open**.

Your friend now receives notification of the file sent. He can choose to accept or decline the file. If he accepts, he can then open or download the file to his computer.

Inviting Others for a Group Chat

Here's another neat feature of Google+ Chat. You can do group chats, where you chat in real time with multiple friends. There's no limit to the number of people you can chat with simultaneously, either, which opens up a number of interesting possibilities.

To start a group chat, follow these steps:

1. Start a chat with a single friend, as described previously.
2. Once you've started the chat, click the **Start Group Chat** button at the top of the chat window.
3. The chat window now expands, as shown in Figure 10.6. Enter the names of the contacts you want to add to the chat into the Add People to This Chat box, then press **Enter**.

Figure 10.6: *Inviting others to a group chat.*

Messages from these new contacts will now appear in the chat window.

If you want to exit from a group chat, just close the chat window as you would normally. The others in the chat will see a message that you've left the conversation. If you want to rejoin, you'll need to be re-invited by someone still in the chat. The group chat itself continues until all participants have left.

Viewing Your Chat History

By default, Google+ saves copies of all your chats. Some users like this ability to revisit a chat history, just in case something important got discussed that you'd like to refer to again.

Each complete chat session is saved as a message in your Gmail account. To view your chats, go to your Gmail page (www.gmail.com) and click the **Chats** link in the navigation sidebar. Click a chat to read the history, or delete the chats that you don't really want to keep.

GOOGLE+ PLUS

If you want more privacy, you can go "off the record" during any chat and halt the history recording. All you have to do is click the **Actions** button in that chat window and select **Go Off the Record**. To resume recording the chat history, click the **Actions** button again and select **Go On the Record**. Once you go off the record with a given user, all your subsequent chats—for this and other users—will be off the record until you choose to go on the record again.

Changing Your Status—and Signing Out

By default, Google+ lists you as "available" when you're online and signed in. This tells your friends that you're online and available to chat.

To change your online status, click the **Available** link in the chat section of your home page. As you can see in Figure 10.7, you can then choose from the following statuses: Available, Busy, or Invisible. You can also choose to sign out of chat completely.

Figure 10.7: *Changing your chat status.*

Participating in a Voice Chat

If you have a microphone and speakers installed in your computer, or if you have some form of headset attached, you can use Google+ for voice chats. These free internet-based voice chats can take the place of expensive long-distance telephone calls.

To start a voice chat, follow these steps:

1. Start a regular text-based chat, as described previously.
2. Click the **Start Voice Chat** (telephone) button at the top of the chat window.
3. The other person in the chat will be prompted to answer the call, as shown in Figure 10.8. When he or she answers, start talking!

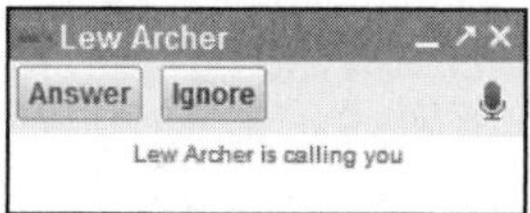

Figure 10.8: *Starting a voice chat.*

To end a voice chat, simply click the **End** button that appears at the top of the chat window.

GOOGLE+ INSIDER

You can only do one-on-one voice chats; Google+ doesn't allow group voice chats.

The Least You Need to Know

- Google+ offers three types of real-time chat: text, voice, and video.
- You have to invite friends to join your Google+ Chat List.
- Google+ text chat is just like instant messaging, except you can invite multiple friends for a group chat.
- You start a voice chat from within the normal text chat window.

Video Chatting in Hangouts

Chapter

11

In This Chapter

- Participating in a one-on-one video chat
- Creating a hangout for group video chatting
- What goes on in a hangout—and inviting others to hang out
- Going more interactive with Hangouts with Extras
- Broadcasting a hangout across the web with Hangouts on Air

In Chapter 10 I explained how to participate in text and voice chats with your Google+ contacts. That's great, but what if what you really want is to see the person you're talking to?

To that end, Google+ also offers video chats, where you can hold face-to-face conversation with your friends, family members, and business colleagues. In fact, you can even participate in group video chats with up to 10 friends, thanks to Google+'s new hangouts feature. It's just like using Skype, except it's totally free!

Understanding Video Chat—and Hangouts

Text chatting (a.k.a. instant messaging) is great and a rather efficient way to communicate with friends and co-workers. But sometimes you need to talk face-to-face—which is where Google+'s video chat comes in.

If you and a friend both have webcams built into or attached to your computers, you can participate in video chats via Google+. A video chat is just what you think it is, talking to someone in real time over your computer, live picture included. It's the same sort of thing you get from commercial services such as Skype, but it's totally free.

Video chatting is great for both personal and professional use. Personally, I like video chatting with my grandkids; it's almost (but not quite) as good as being there, and a lot more fun than a phone call or voice chat.

Professionally, a lot of businesspeople are using video chat for sales calls and other formerly live meetings. Video chat is faster than email, more personal than instant messaging, and cheaper than making a phone call. With just a few clicks of the mouse, you're having a productive meeting.

Also popular in the business environment are group video chats, sometimes called video conferences. Instead of flying people in from multiple locations to attend a meeting, you hold the meeting via computer, instead. Everybody signs on and participates using their PCs' webcams; it's fast and cheap and very effective.

You can create group video chats using Google+'s innovative hangouts feature. A hangout is essentially a multi-user video chat room in your web browser. You start the chat, invite up to 10 friends or colleagues, and then start talking. Everybody sees everybody else in their own little chat window, so it's pretty much the same feel as a live meeting. The only difference is that each participant is on their own computer in their own location. The hangout stays open until the last participant leaves.

As you might suspect, hangouts are seeing lots of use among the business crowd; free video conferences are understandably popular when companies are cutting their travel budgets. But you can also use hangouts to talk with multiple family members at the same time, conduct neighborhood meetings, or hold student study groups. They're free and easy to set up—all you need is a computer and a webcam for each participant. You can learn more about the many interesting uses for Google+'s group video chat in Chapter 21.

Participating in a Video Chat

Before we delve into the whole hangout thing, let's start with the simpler one-on-one video chat. It's easy to do, assuming that both you and your friend have webcams installed in or attached to your computers. All you have to do is start a normal text chat and then click the **Start Video Chat** button.

To start a video chat, follow these steps:

1. Go to the Google+ home page, scroll to the chat list (in the lower-left corner), and click the name of the person you want to chat with.

GOOGLE+ PLUS

Contacts who are available for video chat (that is, who have active webcams) are listed with a green camera icon in the chat list.

2. When the Chat window opens for a normal text chat, click the **Start Video Chat** (video camera) button at the top of the window, as shown in Figure 11.1.

Figure 11.1: *Click the video camera button to start a video chat.*

3. The other person in the chat will be prompted to answer the request, as shown in Figure 11.2. When your friend accepts the request, the video chat begins.

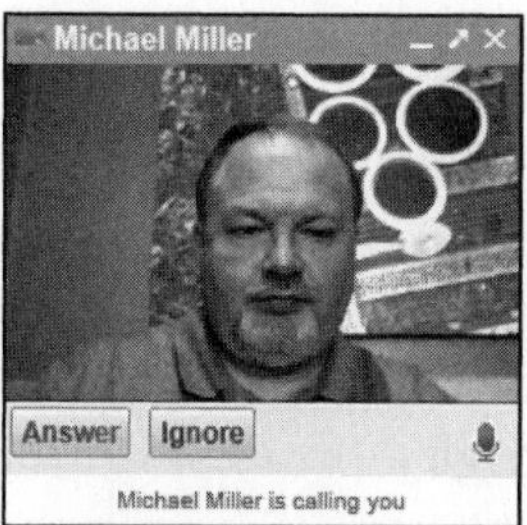

Figure 11.2: *Starting a video chat.*

You're now chatting—feel free to talk as long as you'd like. To end a video chat, just click the **End** button.

Chatting in a Larger Window

By default, the video chat takes place in a small box at the top of the normal chat window. As you can see in Figure 11.3, the person you're talking to appears in the large box. You appear in the smaller box in the lower-right corner of the screen.

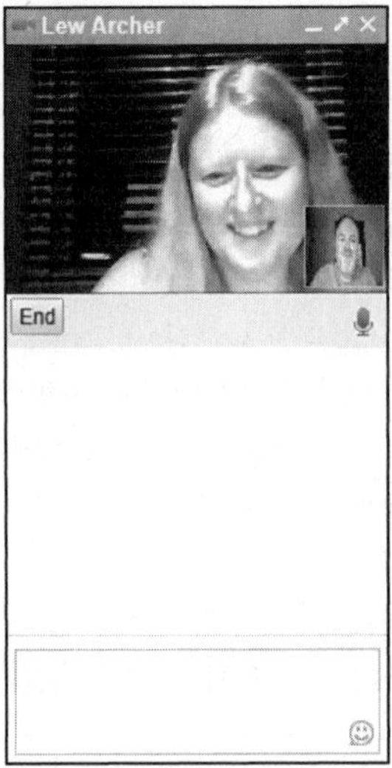

Figure 11.3: *A video chat in progress.*

If you'd rather see a larger picture of whom you're talking to, click the **Pop-Out** (diagonal arrow) button in the chat window. This opens a separate video chat window. You can resize the new window as you like by dragging the corners of the window in or out.

If you'd rather chat full-screen, you can do that, too. Just move your cursor over the chat window and click the icon in the upper-left corner.

Participating in a Group Video Chat

Google+'s normal video chat feature enables one-on-one chat only; you can't chat with multiple people there. If want to do a group chat, you have to create a hangout.

A hangout is simply a group video chat room; it's a way to do multi-user video conferences online for free. A hangout can have up to 10 participants, and stays open until the last person leaves.

Creating a Hangout

To create a hangout for a group video chat, follow these steps:

1. Go to the Google+ home page and click the **Start a Hangout** button in the right column.
2. The Google Hangouts window, shown in Figure 11.4, now appears. (Well, it may take a few moments to appear; Google has to recognize and adjust for your specific video hardware.) The main display in this window shows you a picture of yourself, live on your own webcam.

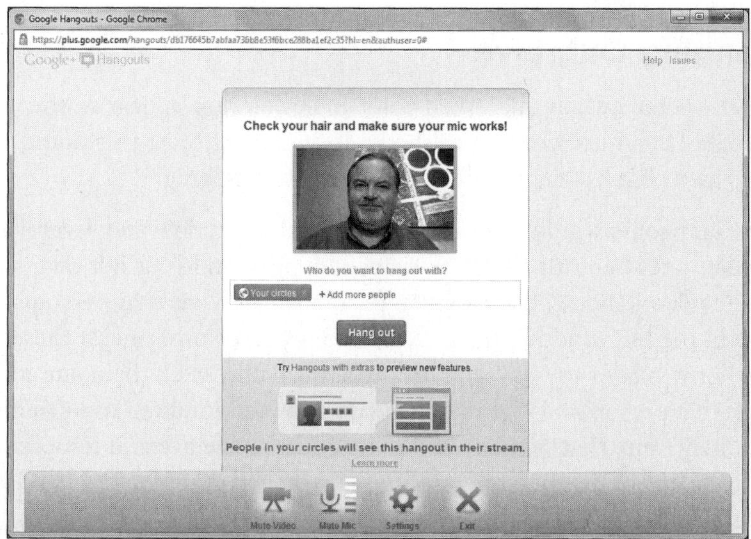

Figure 11.4: *Starting a group video hangout.*

3. A new hangout, by default, is set to include everyone in all your circles. You probably don't want to do this, so click the **X** in the Your Circles box.
4. Now you have to invite some people to your hangout. Click the **Add Circles or People to Share With** link and select the circles of people you want to add to your video chat.
5. You can also invite individual people to your video chat. Just enter one or more names into the **Add More People** box.
6. You're now ready to open your hangout. Click the **Hang Out** button.

Any person you've invited to "hang out" receives an invitation in their Google+ Stream, as shown in Figure 11.5. They can join the hangout by clicking the **Join This Hangout** button.

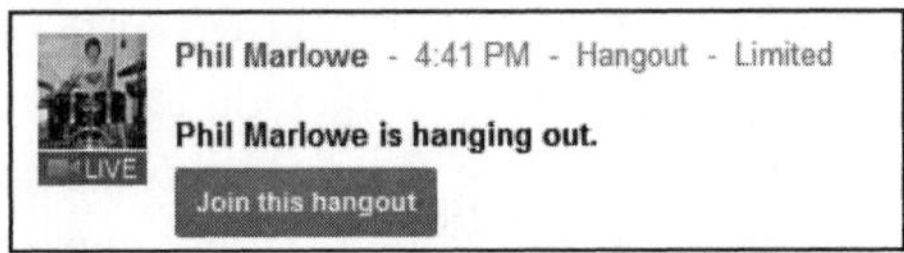

Figure 11.5: *Viewing an invitation to hang out.*

Hanging Out, Live

All the people who've accepted your invitation now appear in the Google Hangouts window, as shown in Figure 11.6. At this point, the video chat has begun and it's time to start talking.

The Hangouts window consists of a big video window and several smaller ones beneath. Each participant appears in his or her own small video window; click a given participant to view that person also in the big window above. Hover your cursor over one of these smaller windows to view that participant's name; click the name to view that person's profile in your main browser window. You can also remotely mute that person's audio, by clicking the green microphone button. And if that person is acting up, you can click the red hand button to report an abuse of privileges to Google.

Figure 11.6: *A group video chat, in progress.*

In addition, you can perform any of the following actions while the hangout is in process:

- Invite additional people to the hangout by clicking the **Invite** icon. This opens the Invite More People pane, shown in Figure 11.7. Click the **Add Circles or People** link and select a circle, or enter individual names within this box. Click the **Invite** button to send the invitations.

Figure 11.7: *Inviting more people to your hangout.*

- Conduct a simultaneous text chat by clicking the **Chat** icon. This opens the Chat pane, shown in Figure 11.8. This is your normal Google+ Chat; type your messages in the box at the bottom and view the ongoing conversation in the main part of the pane.

Figure 11.8: *A group video chat, in progress.*

- View a YouTube video within the video chat by clicking the **YouTube** icon. This displays a large YouTube pane in the main part of the Hangouts window, as shown in Figure 11.9. Use the Search box to search for a video, which then starts playing for all participants. (You can, by the way, talk to participants while a YouTube video is playing; just click and hold the **Push to Talk** button and then say something.)

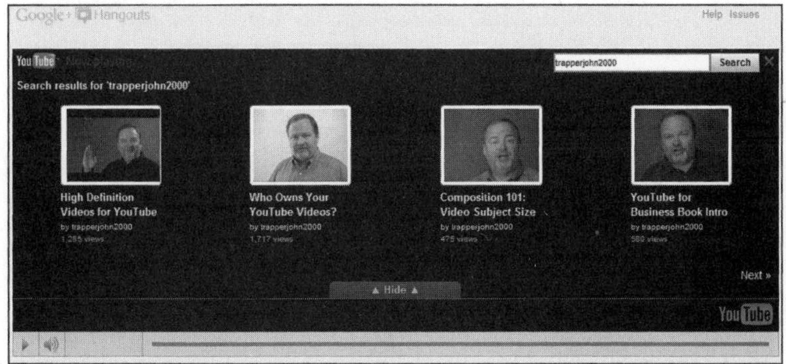

Figure 11.9: *Choosing a YouTube video to view in your hangout.*

- Temporarily "mute" your video stream by clicking the **Mute Video** icon—this causes your picture to go blank on everyone else's computer. Click this button again to return to live video.
- Mute your microphone by clicking the **Mute Mic** icon; click it again to turn on your mic.
- Adjust various hangout settings by clicking the **Settings** icon. (We'll discuss these in a moment.)
- Exit from the video chat by clicking the **Exit** icon.

It's pretty straightforward, all things considered. The Hangouts window stays open even when individual participants leave. The last person to exit effectively closes the hangout.

Adjusting Hangout Settings

I mentioned hangout settings. When you click the **Settings** button in the Hangouts window, you see the Settings panel shown in Figure 11.10. Basically, you use the Settings panel to select or adjust the webcam, microphone, and speakers you're using for the video conference.

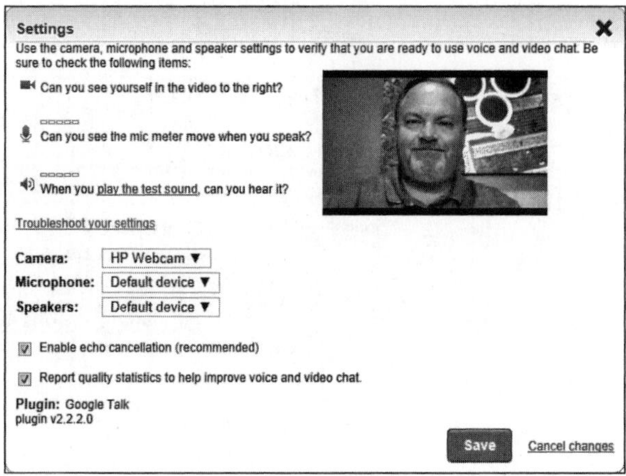

Figure 11.10: *Adjusting settings for your hangout.*

If everything is adjusted properly, you should be able to see yourself in the video preview window at the top right, see the mic meter move when you talk, and hear the test tone when you click the link. If you can't, then make other selections from the Camera, Microphone, or Speakers lists. Click the **Save** button when you're done.

GOOGLE+ MINUS

On some systems you may hear an echo of your own voice when you talk. If this is the case, check the **Enable Echo Cancellation** box in the Settings panel.

Using Hangouts with Extras

So far we've been examining Google+'s standard hangouts. There's also a version of hangouts with extra features, imaginatively dubbed Hangouts with Extras, that you might want to investigate.

GOOGLE+ INSIDER

Google is using Hangouts with Extras to test features that it hopes to eventually add to the regular version of hangouts. It's possible that, by the time you read this, some or all of the features described here will be incorporated into regular hangouts.

To use Hangouts with Extras, go to the Google+ home page and click the **Start a Hangout** button. When the Google+ Hangouts window appears, click the **Hangouts with Extras** link.

What new extra features are available? Let's look at them.

Naming Your Hangout

The default version of hangouts creates unnamed video chats. Hangouts with Extras, on the other hand, lets you name your chats. This is great if you're creating a public hangout on a specific topic; just name your hangout appropriately.

You name your hangout when you first create it. The new Welcome to Google+ Hangouts with Extras window, shown in Figure 11.11, prompts you to enter a hangout name. (Along with those participants you want to invite, of course.) Just enter the name into the Hangout name box and proceed from there.

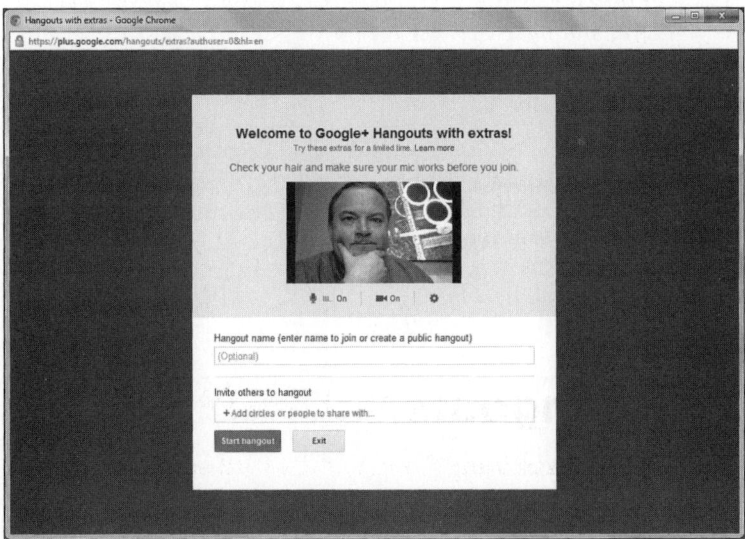

Figure 11.11: *Naming a new hangout.*

The new Hangouts with Extras window looks a little different from the regular hangouts window, by the way. As you can see in Figure 11.12, participants are displayed along the right side of the screen, the main presenter or presentation is in the middle, and the left sidebar is used for text chat, notes, and navigation. There are also some useful buttons along the top of the window. We'll discuss the most useful of these in due course.

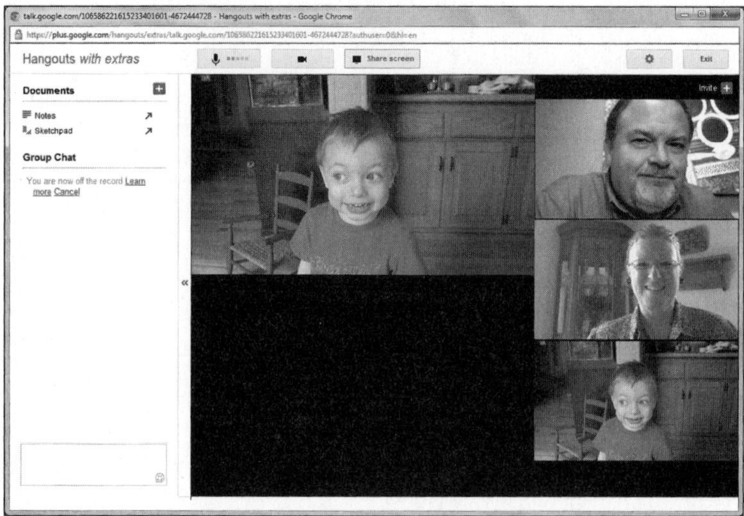

Figure 11.12: *The new Hangouts with Extras window.*

GOOGLE+ MINUS

One thing you lose when you switch to Hangouts with Extras is the ability to view and share YouTube videos within a video chat. Other than that, you retain all the existing features, while adding these new ones.

Sharing Notes

Ever want to jot down a few random notes while participating in a video conference. Now you can. Hangouts with Extras includes a Notes feature, which lets you do just that.

To create a note, click the **Notes** link in the left navigation sidebar. Since notes are actually shared documents, Google+ needs your permission to create and share the note. When prompted, click the **Open** button.

A note window now opens in the middle of your hangout window, as shown in Figure 11.13. This works like any word processor; just start typing, and use the formatting controls as necessary.

Figure 11.13: *Creating a note.*

Once you create a note, others in the hangout can view it. All they have to do is click the Notes link in their own hangout window, and they'll see what you've written.

Sharing a Sketchpad

You're not limited to creating and sharing written notes. Thanks to Google's Sketchpad drawing app, you can also share drawings, doodles, pictures, and other images. Just click the **Sketchpad** link in the left navigation sidebar to display the Sketchpad app in the hangout window. As you can see in Figure 11.14, you can draw various lines and shapes, add text boxes and web links, insert image files, and so forth. It's great for visual communicators.

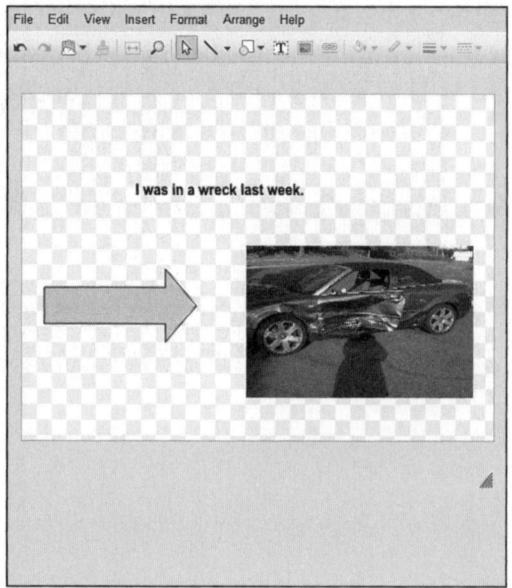

Figure 11.14: *Communicating visually with Sketchpad.*

Sharing Google Docs

You can also use Hangouts with Extras to share word processing documents, spreadsheets, or presentations with other participants. In particular, you can share and collaborate on any type of Google Docs document in the hangout window.

It's relatively easy to do. Just click the **+** button next to the Documents section in the left navigation sidebar. You now see the Select Document to Share pane; select a document from the list and click the **Select** button. The document now appears in the main part of the hangout window, as shown in Figure 11.15.

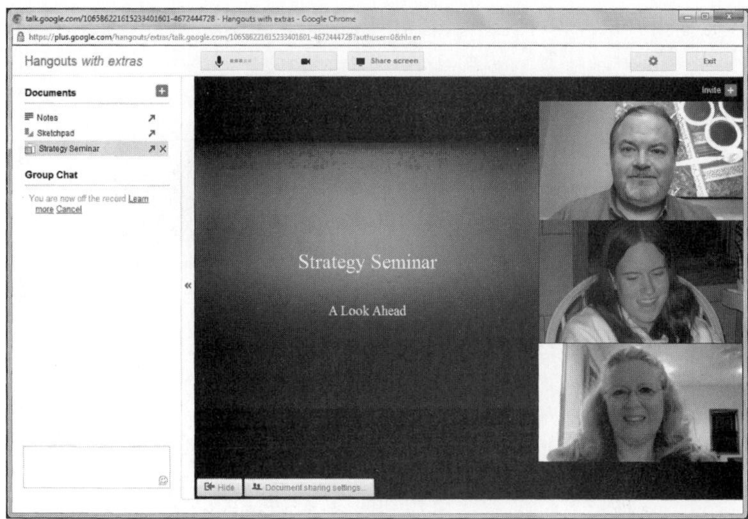

Figure 11.15: *Viewing a Google Docs presentation in a hangout.*

By default, participants can only view the documents you display—which is fine for presentations. If you want participants to be able to edit and collaborate on a document, click the **Sharing Settings** button below the document onscreen; when the Sharing Settings dialog box appears, enter the participants' names into the Add People box, and select **Can Edit** for each collaborator.

Sharing Your Screen

While we're talking about sharing, you can now opt to share your entire screen with participants in your hangout. This way you can let participants see what you're working on or viewing on your computer, on their computers. You can choose to share your entire computer desktop or individual open windows.

To share your screen, click the **Share Screen** button at the top of the hangout window. When the Google Talk Screen Sharing Request window appears, as shown in Figure 11.16, click what you want to share, then click the **Share Selected Window** button. The shared item now appears in place of your normal webcam display in the hangout window.

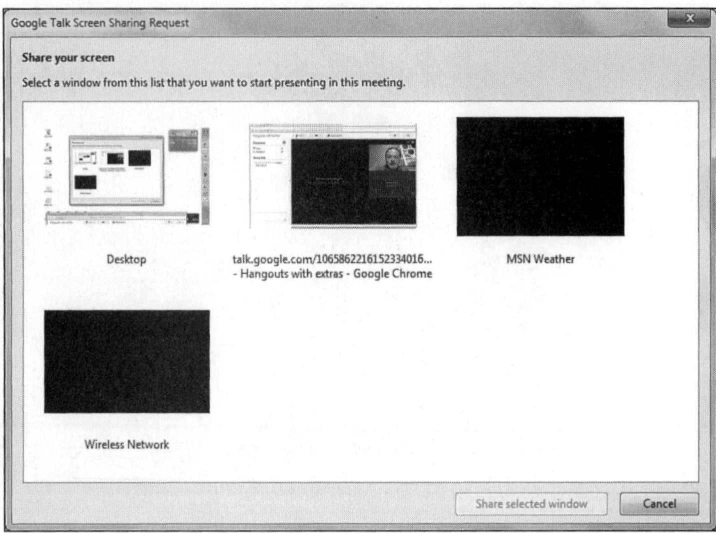

Figure 11.16: *Selecting what to share.*

GOOGLE+ PLUS

If you have a smart phone, you can participate in video hangouts while you're on the go via the Google+ mobile app. Learn more in Chapter 16.

Broadcasting a Hangout

As noted, hangouts are limited to ten participants. You can, however, broadcast your hangout to a larger group of viewers (who just watch and can't interact) via Google+'s Hangouts on Air feature. A Hangout on Air is publicly webcast over the internet to anyone who wants to watch, and archived on YouTube for future viewing.

Why might you want to broadcast your hangout in this fashion? Well, if you want more than ten people to view it, this is the only way to go. That makes it ideal for large company meetings, industry conferences, press conferences, even music concerts and other live performances.

GOOGLE+ PLUS

Hangout on Air viewers can only view the main participant or presentation in a hangout. They cannot switch views, participate in text chat, edit notes and documents, or otherwise interact with the session.

At present, Hangouts on Air are available only to selected users. (If you're selected, you'll see an option to broadcast and record your hangout when you first launch it.) Any Google+ user, however, can join a broadcast hangout as a viewer.

The Least You Need to Know

- Video chat lets you see who you're talking to—it's a live audio/video conversation in real time.
- Google+'s Hangout feature lets you host group video chats with up to 10 friends.
- Hangout invitations appear in the invitee's stream.
- While you're in a hangout, you can text chat with participants and watch YouTube videos.
- The hangout stays open until the last person leaves.
- Hangouts with Extras add more interactive features to a hangout, including shared notes, sketches, documents, and screens.
- You can also broadcast a hangout to multiple non-participating viewers with Hangouts on Air.

Sharing with Google+

Part 3

Everyone wants to share, right? Whether you like to share a lot of things or just a few, Google+ is all about sharing, and so is this part.

When it comes to sharing, it's nice to be able to post a picture of your latest family gathering, night out on the town, or a recent vacation to let others see what you have been up to lately. With Google+, you can share your digital photos, vacation videos or home movies, or even stuff you simply find interesting on the web. Why hold back?

In the spirit of all of this sharing, I'll share with you how Google+ lets you manage and edit multiple photo albums, tag photos, and download friends' photos. You'll also learn about uploading videos, finding friends' videos, and even deleting videos.

Sharing Photos

Chapter 12

In This Chapter

- Viewing, commenting on, and downloading friends' photos
- Finding photos of yourself on Google+
- Removing your tags from photos
- Uploading photos and creating new photo albums
- Managing your photo albums and editing the photos you upload

Back in Chapter 9, I explained how you can include photos in the posts you make. Posting isn't the only way to share photos on Google+, however. You can upload all the photos you want, organize them into online photo albums, and then share them with members of your circles. You can also view your friends' photo albums, of course.

How do you go about sharing photos on Google+? Read on to find out.

Understanding Google+ Photo Sharing

Photo sharing is one of the most social activities you can do on a social network. People love to look at photos of their friends and families; sharing photos on Google+ is a far sight easier than trying to send multiple photos to multiple recipients via email.

Photo sharing is also where we see the synergy between various Google properties. In this instance, it's because Google+'s photo-sharing feature is tied into Google's *Picasa Web Albums*. In fact, Google+'s photos *are* Picasa Web Albums; if you already have a Picasa account, those photos show up as your Google+ photos.

In Google+/Picasa, the photos you upload are stored in *photo albums*. You can decide which of your circles or friends can view each album you create; this way you can selectively share some pictures with some people but not with others.

DEFINITION

Picasa Web Albums, also known as Google Photos, is Google's online photo-sharing service. It's located at picasaweb.google.com. A **photo album** is a means of storing multiple photos in a single location, like a folder for photos.

You can upload photos from your computer or from your mobile phone. Once you've uploaded a photo, you can tag people who appear in that photo. You can also perform some basic photo editing, to fix or punch up any dodgy photos you've taken.

And, of course, you can use Google+ to view photos taken by your Google+ friends. You can view their photo albums just as they can view yours; you can even comment on their photos, as you would a normal post to their stream.

Viewing Friends' Photos

Let's start with viewing friends' photos, which are organized into individual photo albums. You can view any photo in an album that a friend has opted to share with you; that means you may not see all the photos a given friend has uploaded.

Viewing Photos and Albums

To view friends' photos, follow these steps:

1. Click the **Photos** button at the top of any Google+ page.
2. You now see the Photos page. By default, the Photos from Your Circles tab is selected, as shown in Figure 12.1. This page lists the photo albums most recently modified by people in your circles. Click an album to view the photos within.

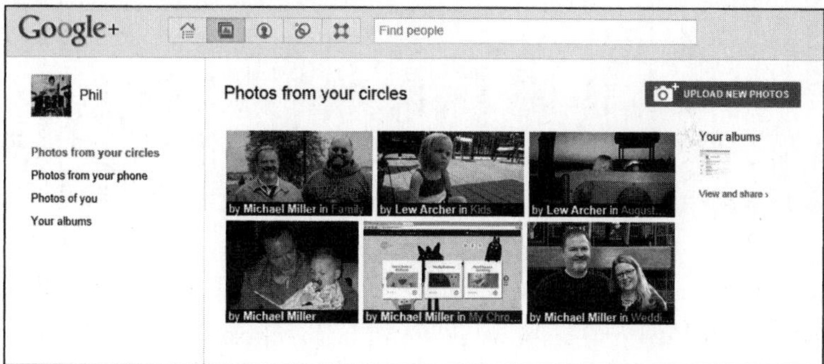

Figure 12.1: *Viewing friends' photo albums on your Photos page.*

GOOGLE+ PLUS

Your Photos page only displays the photo albums most recently modified by your friends. You can view all the photo albums for a given friend by going to that person's profile page and then clicking the **Photos** tab.

3. You now see the main photo in that album displayed in what Google+ calls a *Light Tray*, as shown in Figure 12.2. Click the left or right arrows to go to the previous or next photos, or click any thumbnail beneath the main photo to view that photo.

Figure 12.2: *Viewing a photo in the Light Tray.*

4. To view details about a given photo, click the **Actions** button and select **Photo Details**. This displays the Details pane, shown in Figure 12.3. Here you can view any *metadata* captured when the photo was shot, such as resolution (dimensions), camera used, exposure settings, and so forth.

DEFINITION

The **Light Tray** is the photo viewing pane used in Google+. **Metadata** is information that describes the contents of a file, such as a digital photo. Note that not all digital cameras capture metadata, so you might not see all possible details about a given photo.

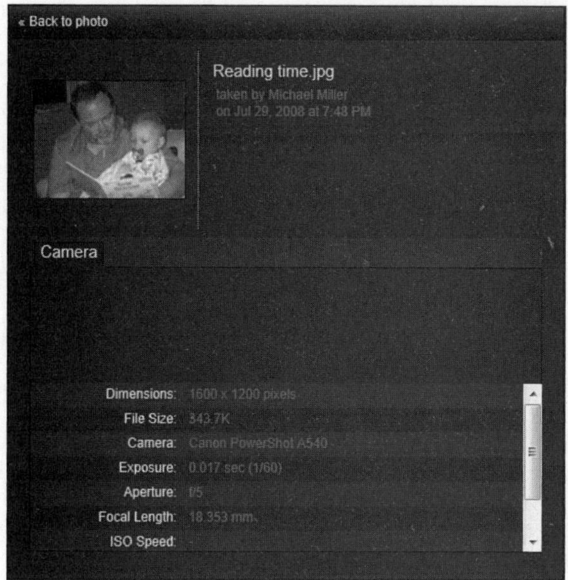

Figure 12.3: *Viewing photo details.*

5. To close the Light Tray and return to the Photos page, click the **X** above the top right side of the photo.

Commenting on a Photo

Since photo sharing is a social activity, Google+ lets you comment on your friends photos. Here's how to do it:

1. Open a friends' photo album and display a given picture.
2. The sidebar on the right, shown in Figure 12.4, displays any comments made by other users. To add your own comment, begin typing into the **Add a Comment** box.
3. Click the **Post Comment** button to post your comment.

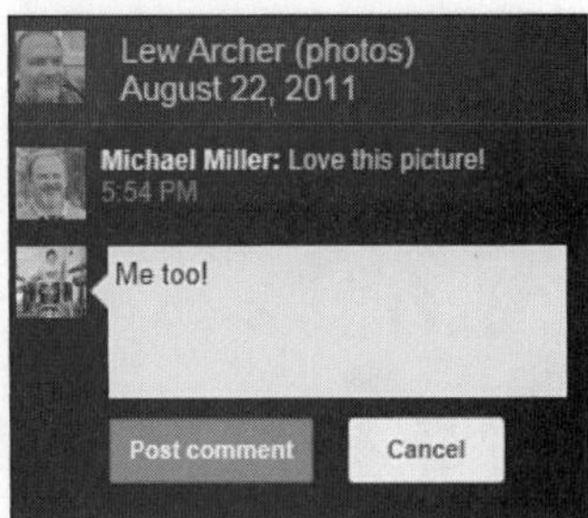

Figure 12.4: *Viewing and adding comments to a photo.*

Your comment appears in the Comments pane for that picture, as well as in your friend's stream, as shown in Figure 12.5.

Figure 12.5: *Viewing photo comments in the stream.*

Downloading a Photo

At present, Google+ doesn't include a button or link to let you download the pictures you view online. However, you can use your web browser's "save picture" functionality to download any Google+ picture to your computer.

Here's how to do it:

1. Display the picture you want to download.
2. Right-click on the picture and select **Save Picture As** or **Save Image As** from the pop-up menu.

3. When the Save Picture or Save As dialog box appears, select a location for the saved picture, then click the **Save** button.

The picture file will be saved in the location you specified.

Tagging a Photo

If you find a friend's photo that contains someone you know, or even yourself, you can tag the people in that photo. When a person is tagged in a photo, that photo will appear on their own Photos page.

To tag a friend's photo, follow these steps:

1. Open a friends' photo album and display a given picture.
2. Hover over a face in the photo; a box appears around the face, as shown in Figure 12.6.

Figure 12.6: *Identifying a face in a photo.*

GOOGLE+ PLUS

If Google+ doesn't find a face in the photo, no box appears. Instead, click the **Add Tag** button beneath the photo, then enter a person's name into the resulting text box that appears. You can also use this method to tag people who do not appear in a photo, such as the picture's photographer.

3. Click the box to display the text box shown in Figure 12.7.

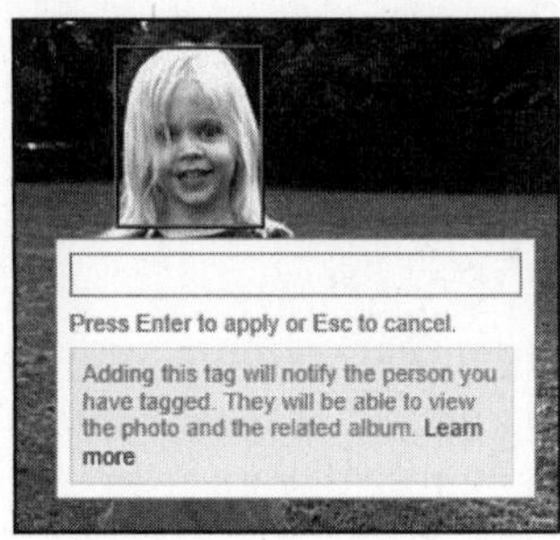

Figure 12.7: *Tagging a friend in a photo.*

4. Start to enter the person's name into the text box; Google+ will suggest a list of friends.
5. Choose a person from the list of suggestions, or finish typing the person's name and press **Enter**.

The person's name you entered will now be tagged in the photo. People tagged in a photo are listed at the bottom of the Comments pane. The friends you tagged are also notified by Google that they've been tagged; they can then choose to keep or remove the tag, as they wish.

Viewing Photos of You

Want to see all the photos in which you appear? Well, as long as you've been tagged in a photo, it's easy enough to display those photos in which you've been tagged. Here's how:

1. Click the **Photos** button at the top of any Google+ page.
2. Click the **Photos of You** tab in the left sidebar.

You now see all the photos in which you've been tagged, as shown in Figure 12.8. These can include photos you have uploaded yourself, as well as photos uploaded by members of your circles.

Figure 12.8: *Viewing photos of you on Google+.*

Removing a Tag

What do you do if you don't want to be tagged in a photo? It can happen; maybe it's an embarrassing photo that you'd rather not be identified with. In any case, Google+ provides a number of opportunities to remove unwanted tags of yourself in friends' photos.

Dealing with a Tag Notification

When you're tagged in a photo, Google+ notifies you and gives you the opportunity to remove the tag. Go to your home page and click the **Notifications** link in the left column to view pending notifications, like the one shown in Figure 12.9. Click the **green check mark** to approve the tag, or click the **X** to remove the tag.

Figure 12.9: *Approving or removing a tag.*

Removing a Tag After the Fact

You can remove a tag from a photo at any time. All you have to do is follow these steps:

1. Display the photo in which you're tagged.
2. Hover over your face to display the tag box around your face, as shown in Figure 12.10.
3. Click the **X** at the top right corner of the box.
4. When prompted to confirm the tag removal, click the **OK** button.

Figure 12.10: *Getting ready to remove a tag.*

Uploading Photos to Google+

Viewing friends' photos is fun, but your friends probably would like to see your photos, too. Let's take a look, then, at how you can share your photos via Google+.

GOOGLE+ INSIDER

You can upload photos at any resolution to Google+, although higher resolution photos will be automatically downsized to no more than 2048 × 2048 pixels. Google+ will accept photos in most popular file formats, including JPG, GIF, and PNG.

Uploading to a New Photo Album

When you upload a photo, you have the option of uploading to a new photo album or uploading to one that you previously created. Let's look at the first option first.

Follow these steps:

1. Click the **Photos** button at the top of any Google+ page.
2. When the Photos page appears, click the **Upload New Photos** button.
3. When the Upload and Share Photos pane appears, as shown in Figure 12.11, enter a name for the new photo album into the Album Name box. (If you don't enter a name, Google+ names it with today's date.)

Figure 12.11: *Creating a new photo album.*

4. Click the **Select Photos from Your Computer** button.

GOOGLE+ PLUS

If you're using Firefox or Google's Chrome web browser, you also have the option of dragging and dropping photos directly onto the Upload and Share Photos pane.

5. When the Choose File to Upload or Open dialog box appears, navigate to and select the photos you want to upload, then click the **Open** button.
6. The photos you selected now appear in the Upload and Share Photos pane. Click the **Upload More** link to upload additional photos.
7. Click the **Create Album** button.
8. You now see the Share Album pane, shown in Figure 12.12. Enter a description of this album into the top text box.

Figure 12.12: *Sharing a new photo album.*

9. Click the **Add Circles or People to Share With** link to select which circles or individuals you want to view this album.
10. Click the **Share** button.

Your photos now appear in the new photo album you created. Note that a Google+ Photo Album can contain up to 1,000 pictures.

Uploading to an Existing Photo Album

You probably don't want to create a new photo album every time you have photos to upload. You may want to create a single "Summer Photos" album, for example, and upload all the photos you take all summer long into this album.

To upload photos to an existing photo album, follow these steps:

1. Click the **Photos** button at the top of any Google+ page.
2. When the Photos page appears, click the **Your Photos** link in the left column.
3. Google+ now displays the Your Albums page, shown in Figure 12.13. Click the album to which you want to add photos.

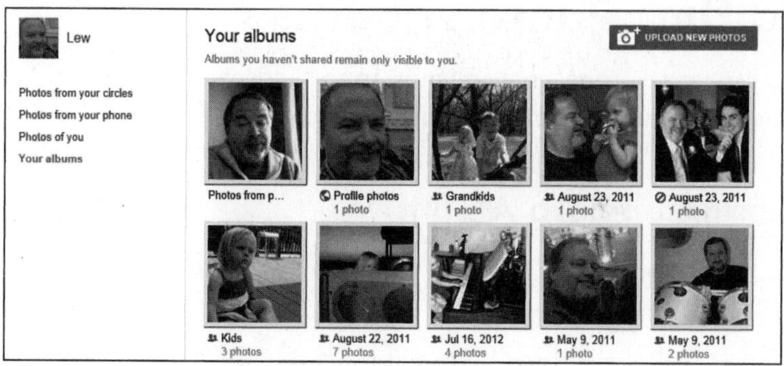

Figure 12.13: *Viewing all your photo albums.*

4. When the album page appears, click the **Add More Photos** button.
5. When the Add Photos to Album pane appears, click the **Select Photos from Your Computer** button.
6. When the Choose File to Upload or Open dialog box appears, navigate to and select the photos you want to upload, then click the **Open** button.

7. The photos you selected now appear in the Add Photos to Album pane. Click the **Upload More** link to upload additional photos.
8. Click the **Add Photos** button.
9. You now see the Share Album pane. Edit the existing description in the top text box, if you like.
10. If you wish, you can change who you're sharing this album with by clicking the **X** on any existing circle or by clicking the **Add More People** link to add new circles.
11. Click the **Share** button.

Your new photos are now added to the existing album.

Editing Photo Albums

You can, at any time, change who can see a given photo album. You can also delete entire photo albums, and all their contents.

Sharing a Photo Album

To change the sharing status of a given photo album, follow these steps:

1. Click the **Photos** button at the top of any Google+ page.
2. When the Photos page appears, click the **Your Albums** link in the left column.
3. When the Your Albums page appears, click the album you want to edit.
4. When the album page appears, click the **Share Album** button.
5. When the Share Album pane appears, click the **X** on any existing circle to remove viewing privileges for members of that circle.

6. Click the **Add More People** link to add new circles or individuals.

7. Click the **Share** button when done.

Deleting a Photo Album

When you remove a photo album, you also remove all the photos that were in that album. Here's how to do it:

1. Click the **Photos** button at the top of any Google+ page.
2. When the Photos page appears, click the **Your Albums** link in the left column.
3. When the Your Albums page appears, click the album you want to edit.
4. When the album page appears, click the **Delete Album** button.
5. When prompted to confirm the deletion, click the **Delete** button.

Editing Photos

Google+ lets you do a bit of editing on any photo you upload. You can tag people in the photo, add a caption to the photo, rotate the picture, or even perform some basic photo editing. Read on to learn more.

Tagging a Photo

To tag a person who appears in a photo, follow these steps:

1. Click the **Photos** button at the top of any Google+ page.
2. When the Photos page appears, click the **Your albums** link in the left column.
3. When the Your Albums page appears, click the album that contains the photo you want to tag.

4. When the album page appears, click the photo you want to tag.
5. Hover over a face in the photo; a box appears around the face.
6. Click the box to display the text box shown in Figure 12.14.

Figure 12.14: *Tagging a person in a photo.*

7. Start to enter the person's name into the text box; Google+ will suggest a list of friends.
8. Choose a person from the list of suggestions, or finish typing the person's name and press **Enter**.

The person's name you entered will now be tagged in the photo.

Adding a Photo Caption

You can also add captions to your photos. These serve to help describe the photo to anyone viewing it. Follow these steps:

1. Display the photo you want to caption.
2. Click within the **Add a Caption** box beneath the photo, as shown in Figure 12.15, and type your caption.
3. Press **Enter** when done.

Figure 12.15: *Adding a caption to a photo.*

Rotating a Photo

Sometimes landscape photos get displayed in portrait mode, and vice versa. To rotate such a sideways picture, follow these steps:

1. Display the photo you want to rotate.
2. Click the **Actions** button.
3. Select **Rotate Left** or **Rotate Right**, as appropriate.

Your photo will now be rotated.

Editing a Photo

Google+ also includes some rudimentary photo editing controls. You can apply the following effects:

Cross process, which gives a blueish tint to black areas of a photo.

Orton, which creates and then blends two versions of the photo to create a high contrast effect.

GOOGLE+ INSIDER

The Orton effect, sometimes called an Orton slide sandwich, produces similar results to high dynamic range (HDR) photography.

I'm feeling lucky, which applies Google's best guess as to fixing your photo.

Black and white, which creates a monochrome version of the photo.

Auto color, which automatically corrects the color values in a photo.

Auto contrast, which automatically corrects the brightness and contrast levels of a photo.

To apply any of these effects, follow these steps:

1. Display the photo you want to edit.
2. Click the **Actions** button.
3. Click **Edit Photo**.
4. Google+ now displays the photo editing pane shown in Figure 12.16. Click the effect you wish to add.
5. To remove an effect you just applied, click the **Undo** button.
6. When you're done editing, click the **Done Editing** button.

Figure 12.16: *Applying photographic effects to a picture.*

Deleting a Photo

Finally, you can remove any photo you've uploaded. Just follow these steps:

1. Display the photo you want to delete.
2. Click the **Actions** button.
3. Select **Delete Photo**.
4. When prompted to confirm the deletion, click **OK**.

The photo is now deleted.

The Least You Need to Know

- Google+ works in conjunction with Picasa Web Albums to store digital photos online.
- You can select which circles and individuals can view the photos you upload.
- Your uploaded photos are stored in photo albums; each album can contain up to 1,000 photos.
- You can tag any person who appears in a photo.
- You can also apply selected effects to any photo you upload.

Chapter 13

Sharing Videos

In This Chapter

- Finding and viewing videos from your friends
- Uploading your own videos to Google+
- Deleting videos you've uploaded

Just as you can share photos in Google+, you can also share videos—home movies or whatever you upload and then let your friends watch. Naturally, you can view videos uploaded by your friends, as well.

So how do you do the video sharing thing? It's easy, as you'll soon discover.

Viewing Friends' Videos

Let's start with the easy part—watching videos that your friends have uploaded to Google+.

Finding and Viewing a Video

When a friend uploads a video to Google+, it's displayed on the Videos tab of their profile page. Here's how to find and view a friend's videos:

1. Go to your friend's profile page.
2. Click the **Videos** tab.

3. This displays all the videos your friend has uploaded, as shown in Figure 13.1. Click the video you want to watch.

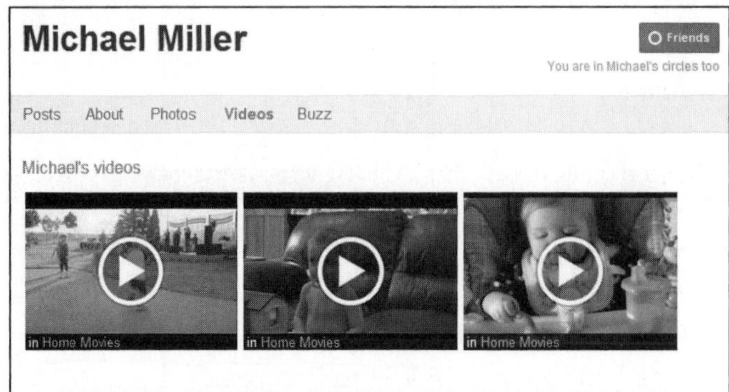

Figure 13.1: *Viewing a friend's videos.*

4. A Light Box page now opens for this video, as shown in Figure 13.2, and video playback begins.

Figure 13.2: *Viewing a video.*

GOOGLE+ PLUS

To view information about a video, click the **Actions** button beneath the video and select **Video Details**.

Controlling Video Playback

You control the video by using the playback controls underneath the video player, as shown in Figure 13.3:

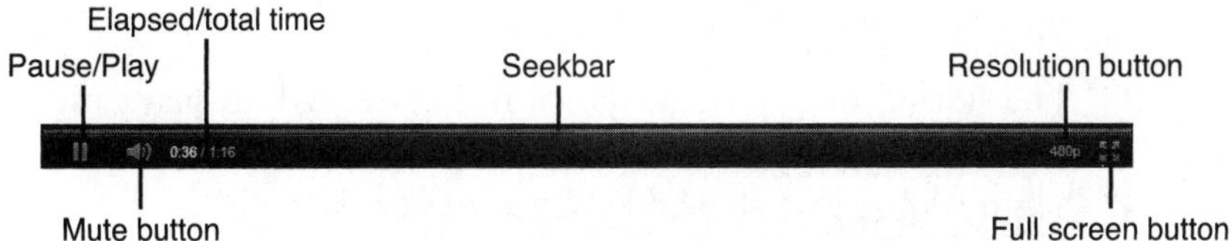

Figure 13.3: *Video playback controls.*

- Click the **Pause** button to pause the video; when paused, the button turns into a Play button. Click the **Play** button to resume playback.
- Click the **Mute** button to mute the sound; click the button again to unmute the sound.
- Hover over the **Mute** button to display the Volume slider. Drag the slider to the left to lower the audio volume; drag it to the right to make it louder.
- Click the **Resolution** button to change the playback *resolution* of the video.
- Click the **Full Screen** button to watch the video on your entire computer screen. Press **Esc** to exit full-screen mode.

Above these controls is the time control, called the *Seekbar*, which indicates the exact time in the video. Drag the slider to the left to view earlier in the video; drag it to the right to advance further into the video. You can also click on the Seekbar to go to a specific point in time.

DEFINITION

Resolution measures the amount of detail in a picture. Higher resolution means a better picture. The **Seekbar** lets you skip directly to a specific point in a video.

Commenting on a Video

You can voice your comments on any videos your friends upload. Here's how to do it:

1. Go to your friend's profile page, open the **Videos** tab, and click on a given video.
2. The sidebar on the right, shown in Figure 13.4, displays any comments made by other users. To add your own comment, begin typing into the **Add a Comment** box.
3. Click the **Post Comment** button to post your comment.

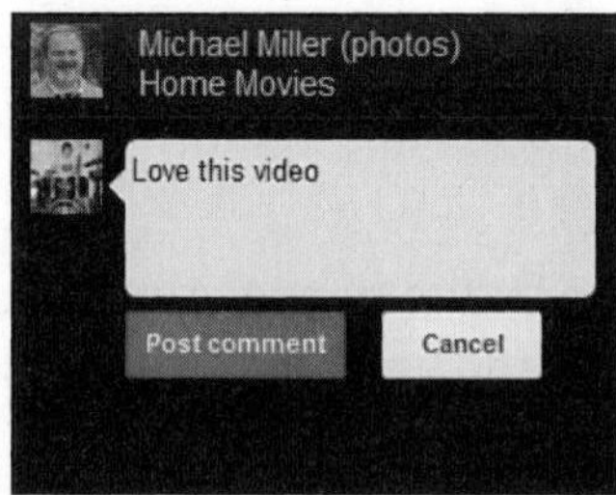

Figure 13.4: *Adding comments to a video.*

Your comment appears in the Comments pane for that picture, as well as in your friend's stream.

Uploading Videos to Google+

It's also rather easy to upload your own videos to Google+. The videos you upload are stored in albums, just like the photos you upload. In fact, Google+'s video sharing is part of its photo-sharing feature; they're both hosted in conjunction with Picasa Web Albums.

You can upload videos in all major video file formats and all resolutions, up to 1080p, and you can upload an unlimited number of videos. The only restriction is that each video can be no more than 15 minutes in length.

To upload a video, follow these steps:

1. Click the **Profile** button at the top of any Google+ page.
2. On your profile page, click the **Videos** tab.
3. From the Videos tab, click the **Upload New Videos** button, shown in Figure 13.5.

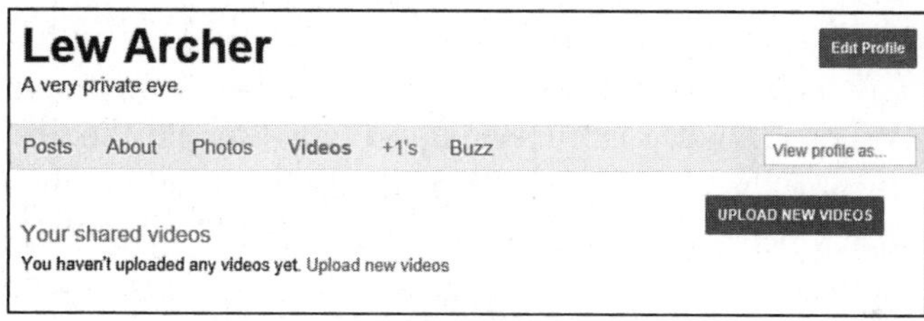

Figure 13.5: *Getting ready to upload a new video.*

4. When the Upload and Share Videos pane appears, as shown in Figure 13.6, you can opt to create a new album for this video or upload it to an existing album. Enter the name of the new album or click the **Add to an Existing Album** link and select the desired album.

Figure 13.6: *Selecting a video to upload.*

5. Click the **Select Videos from Your Computer** button.
6. When the Choose File to Upload or Open dialog box appears, navigate to and select the video you want, then click the **Open** button.
7. The video now begins to upload. Depending on the length of the video and the speed of your internet connection, this may take some time.
8. When the video is finished uploading, Google+ begins processing the video for viewing and displays the thumbnail for that video, as shown in Figure 13.7. Click the **Add Videos** button.

Figure 13.7: *The video has been uploaded.*

9. You now see the Share Album pane, shown in Figure 13.8. Enter a new or edit the existing description in the top text box, if you like.

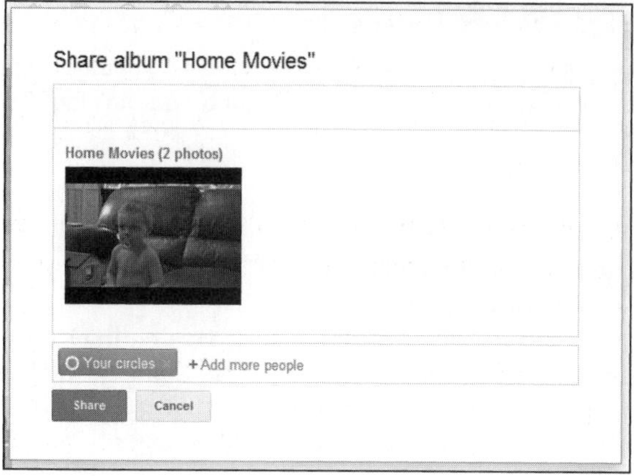

Figure 13.8: *Editing album and sharing information for your video.*

10. If you wish, you can change who you're sharing this album with by clicking the **X** on any existing circle or by clicking the **Add More People** link to add new circles.
11. Click the **Share** button.

The video is now added to the Videos tab on your profile page, as well as posted to your stream, as shown in Figure 13.9. Friends in the circles you specified can now view the video.

Figure 13.9: *An uploaded video, posted to your stream.*

GOOGLE+ INSIDER

Working with videos is similar to working with photos in many respects. However, unlike Google+'s photo sharing, you can't tag or download videos.

Deleting a Video

What if you upload a video you later wish you hadn't? Google+ makes it easy enough to delete any of your videos. Follow these steps:

1. Go to the Videos tab on your profile page.
2. Click the video you want to delete.
3. Click the **Actions** button under the video.
4. Select **Delete Video**.
5. When prompted to confirm the deletion, click the **OK** button.

The Least You Need to Know

- Google+ treats video sharing much as it does photo sharing, including organizing uploaded videos in albums.
- Videos that your friends upload can be found on the Videos tab of their profile page.
- You upload your own videos from the Videos tab of your profile page; you can upload just about any video, up to 15 minutes in length.
- Videos you upload are shared with the circles you select, and posted to your Google+ Stream.

Searching Google+

Chapter 14

In This Chapter

- Understanding Google+ search
- Conducting a Google+ search
- Filtering search results
- Saving your searches

All the posts and uploads and things shared on Google+ combine to create a huge database of information. Since Google is all about the search, it comes as no surprise that you can search Google+ for just about anything that interests you. You can even save those searches, so that you can find new answers to your query with a single click.

Understanding Google+ Search

As you can see in Figure 14.1, there's a search box at the top of every Google+ page. You use this search box to search across Google+ and the web.

Figure 14.1: *The Google+ search box.*

What content is available in a Google+ search? Here's where Google+ gets its search results:

- **Google+ posts.** When you search Google+, you search all the public posts made by Google+ users, as well as those posts that were shared with you. You might be surprised how much useful information is contained in these posts.
- **Google+ users.** A Google+ search also searches the master database of Google+ users, so that people who match your query appear in the search results.
- **Sparks.** A *spark* is how Google refers to trending content that appears on the web. Google+ users create sparks from their saved searches; you can then search the results of these saved searches.

DEFINITION

A **spark** tracks trending web content—a web page relevant to the current query.

Google+ will search all these data sources and return its results in a master search results list. You can then filter the search results to display only posts, people, or sparks.

Conducting a Search

Searching Google+ is as easy as entering a query and viewing the results. Here's how it works:

1. Enter one or more keywords into the search box at the top of any Google+ page.
2. As you type, Google+ displays users whose names match your query. To select one of these users, click the user name, or …
3. Continue entering the rest of your query, then press the **Enter** key.

Google+ now displays a list of matching items, as shown in Figure 14.2. By default, Google+ displays Everything—all types of results in a single list. You can, however, filter the results by source simply by clicking any of the following links located above the search results.

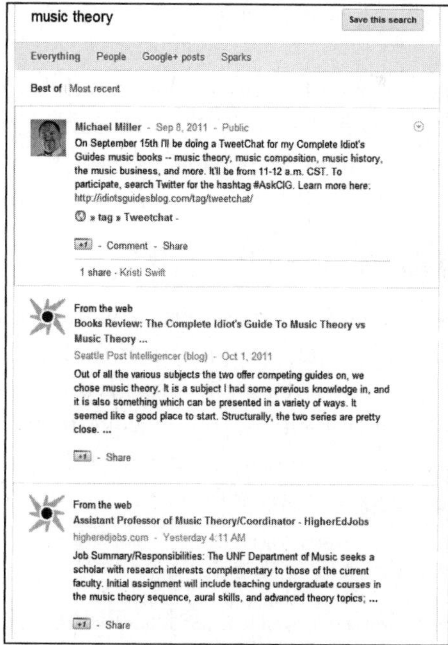

Figure 14.2: *The results of a Google+ search.*

- **Everything**. The default display that lists all search results from all sources.
- **People**. Displays only those Google+ users whose names match your query.
- **Google+ posts**. Displays public posts by other Google+ users, or those posts shared with you, that match your query. In the search results, these items are accompanied by the name and picture of the poster; any comments to the original post are also included.
- **Sparks**. Displays those web pages relevant to your query. These items are accompanied by the sparks logo (looks kind of like a sun) and the words "From the web." Click a link to view the page in its entirety.

GOOGLE+ MINUS

Content from Google+ posts may be relevant and may be interesting, but they're not always true or factual. In other words, you can't always trust what strangers post online.

For all sources except people, Google+ lets you display either the Best Of all results (default) or Most Recent results. Simply click the appropriate link at the top of the results list.

Saving Your Searches

If you're really interested in a given topic, you may find yourself searching for that topic time and time again. Well, instead of conducting each further search manually, Google+ lets you save your searches. You can then re-run a search by clicking a link.

Saving a Search

To save a search, follow these steps:

1. Conduct a Google+ search, as described previously.
2. When the search results page appears, click the **Save This Search** button at the top of the search results page.

Revisiting a Saved Search

All your saved searches are listed in the left-hand sidebar on the Google+ home page, just above the Chat section, as shown in Figure 14.3. To re-run a saved search, all you have to do is click the link to that search. Follow these steps:

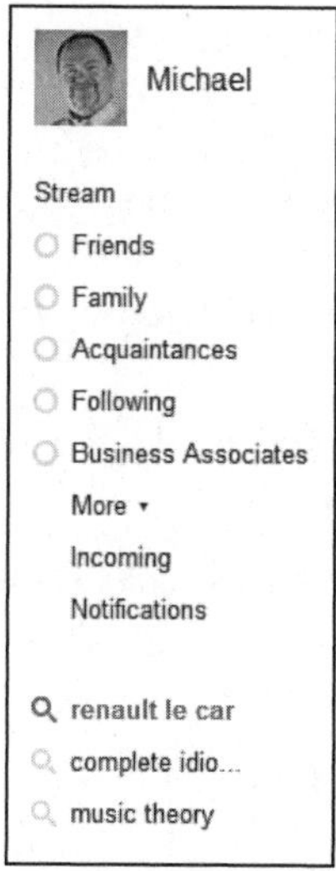

Figure 14.3: *Saved searches in the Google+ sidebar.*

1. Go to your Google+ home page.
2. Scroll to the saved searches section of the left sidebar.
3. Click the search you want to view.

Deleting Saved Searches

What do you do when you're no longer interested in a topic? Well, it's easy enough to delete a saved search. Follow these steps:

1. Go to your Google+ home page.
2. Scroll to the saved searches in the left sidebar.
3. Hover over the search you want to delete.

4. When the X appears, as shown in Figure 14.4, click it.

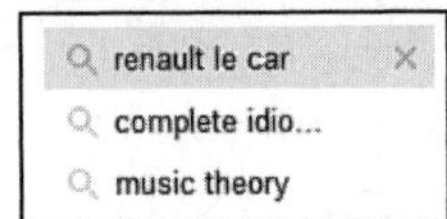

Figure 14.4: *Deleting a saved search.*

The Least You Need to Know

- Google+ lets you search Google+ posts, Google+ users, and web pages.
- You can filter your search results by People, Google+ Posts, and Sparks (web searches).
- You can save Google+ searches for later recall.

Part 4
Using Google+ on the Go

Got a smart phone? Then you can use Google+ from just about anywhere.

In this part, you'll discover the mobile versions of Google+ including the apps available for smart phones and the mobile website version for any web-enabled phone. Keeping in touch on the go has never been simpler and I'll explain all that you can do with Google+ while you are out and about.

That means posting and reading posts in the stream, uploading photos and viewing photo albums, and checking in. You'll also learn about participating in group text chats. I'll explain how to start and participate in these text conversations and even how to control who you invite and who can invite you. I'll also explain how to participate in video chats on your mobile phone, which you can also do with Google+. Who needs a computer, anyway?

Using Google+ on Your Mobile Phone

Chapter

15

In This Chapter

- Discovering the mobile versions of Google+
- Viewing the stream and reading posts using the Google+ mobile app
- Accessing the Google+ mobile website from any web-enabled phone

It's more and more likely these days that you connect to the internet from your mobile phone instead of (or in addition to) your computer. We do a lot of stuff while we're on the go; should social sharing be any different?

To that end, Google has developed mobile versions of Google+ for most major smart phones today. Specifically, there are Google+ apps for Apple's iPhone and Google Android phones that make it easy to use Google+; there's even a mobile version of the Google+ site that you can access from any web-enabled phone.

Understanding Google+ Mobile Version

Facebook has a mobile version, as does Twitter. So it makes sense that Google is focusing on mobile versions of Google+, too. After all, more of us are accessing the web from mobile devices, and we want to do our social networking while we're on the go.

How you access Google+ while you're on the go depends on what type of phone you have. To that end, Google+ has native apps available for the following phones:

- Apple iPhone (iOS 4 and higher)
- Android phones (Android version 2.1 and higher)

You can download each of these apps, for free, from their respective app stores.

For other web-enabled phones (including Windows Mobile and BlackBerry), you can access Google+ using your phone's web browser. Just point your mobile browser to the Google+ mobile website (m.google.com/plus) to delve into the mobile stream.

GOOGLE+ INSIDER

Google+'s mobile availability may change by the time you read this. For example, Google is already rumored to be working on a Google+ app for Windows Phone. Depending on what type of phone you're using, patience may be advised.

Using the Google+ App

If you have an iPhone or an Android phone, you're in luck! You can download and install the Google+ app on your phone, and access Google+ from there. It's the best and easiest way to use Google+ while you're on the go.

Both the iPhone and Android versions of the Google+ app have similar features and functionality—although the Android app tends to be updated a little quicker than the iPhone app. Because of the popularity of the iPhone I'll focus on the iPhone app here, but know if you have the Android version, basic operation isn't that different.

Welcome to the Home Screen

The first time you launch the Google+ app you'll be prompted to sign in to your account, as shown in Figure 15.1. Tap the **Sign In** button and then enter your Google Account email address and password, then click the **Sign In** button. You're now ready to start using Google+ on your mobile phone.

Figure 15.1: *Logging in to Google+.*

GOOGLE+ PLUS

To sign out of your Google+ account, go to the Home screen and tap the **Settings** (gear) button at the top of the screen. When the Settings screen appears, tap **Sign Out**.

What you see when you first log in to the Google+ app is the Google+ home screen. As you can see in Figure 15.2, there are five icons on this screen, for five key Google+ functions.

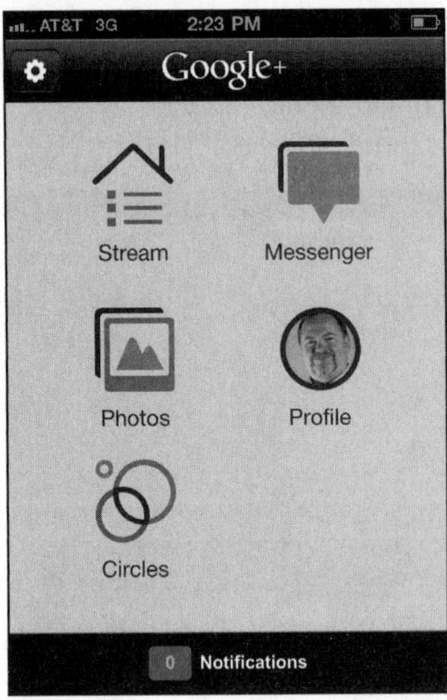

Figure 15.2: *The Google+ home screen.*

- **Stream**. Tap this icon to view your Google+ Stream.
- **Photos**. Tap this icon to view photos from your circles, photos of you, photos from your phone, and your photo albums.
- **Circles**. Tap this icon to view your circles and individual contacts, and then to go to your contacts' profile pages.
- **Messenger**. This is Google+'s group text chat feature. Tap this button to access or initiate group chats.
- **Profile**. Tap this icon to view your Google+ profile.

At the bottom of the home screen is a Notifications area. If you have any pending Google+ Notifications, they're noted here with a white number in a red box indicating how many notifications you have.

Finally, at the top of the home screen is a Settings (gear) icon. Tap this to view and configure your Google+ Mobile Settings.

Reading the Stream

Probably the most common thing we do with Google+ when we're on the go is read the stream of posts from our friends and other contacts. This is easy enough to do; just tap the **Stream** icon on the Google+ home screen.

The Stream screen, shown in Figure 15.3, displays exactly what you think it should—the most recent posts from your Google+ contacts. The default view displays posts from everyone, although you can customize which posts are displayed. Posts can be plain text or include photos, videos, and links.

Figure 15.3: *Viewing the mobile stream.*

To change which posts are displayed in the stream, tap the bar at the top of the Stream screen. This displays the Choose Views screen, shown in Figure 15.4. Tap a circle to view posts from the contacts in that circle; selected circles are displayed with a green checkmark. Tap any checkmark to deselect that circle.

GOOGLE+ INSIDER

To select circles on the Android app, tap the menu key, then tap **Manage Views**.

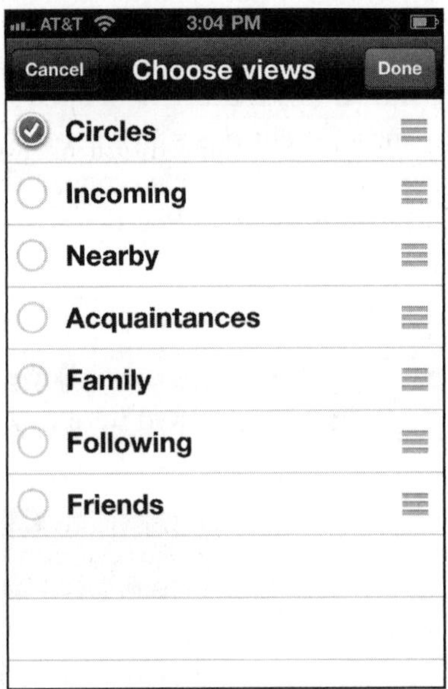

Figure 15.4: *Selecting which circles to view in your mobile stream.*

Once a circle has been selected, it is visible in its own Stream screen. You switch to a different stream by swiping the main stream screen left or right, accordingly. The selected circles are listed at the top of the Stream screen; for example, in Figure 15.3, you see Streams for Circles (currently visible), Nearby (swipe to the left), and Incoming (swipe to the right).

GOOGLE+ PLUS

The Google+ mobile app includes a new noncircle stream titled Nearby. Select this stream to view posts from Google+ users near your current location. This includes users who are not part of your circles or contacts.

If a post includes a photo, tap the photo to view it full-screen. If the post includes a video, tap it to display a video screen. (If you're using the Android app, you can then play the video; you can't yet play videos in the iPhone app.) If the post includes a link, tap the link to go to the linked page.

To return to the home screen, tap the **Home** button at the top left corner of the Stream screen.

Commenting on a Post

It's easy to comment on a post, although not necessarily intuitive. Here's how to do it:

1. Go to the Stream screen.
2. Tap the post you want to comment on.
3. This displays the comments screen, shown in Figure 15.5. All previous comments are listed here.

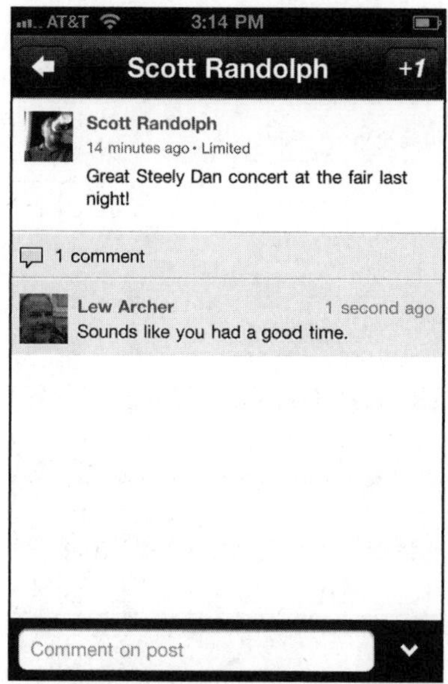

Figure 15.5: *Viewing and making comments.*

4. Tap within the bottom text box.
5. This displays the Comment screen. Type your comment, then tap **Post** to post it.

By the way, you can also +1 any given post. Just tap the post in the stream, then when the Comments screen appears, tap the **+1** button at the top of the screen.

Making a Post

Obviously, you can also use the Google+ app to make your own posts, wherever you may happen to be. Just follow these steps:

1. From the home screen, tap the **Stream** icon.
2. When the Stream screen appears, tap the **Post** (pencil) button at the top of the screen.
3. This displays the Post screen, shown in Figure 15.6. Tap the **Your Circles** button to select which circles you want to post to.

Figure 15.6: *Making a new post.*

4. By default, your current location will be added to your post. If you'd prefer not to show your location, tap the **X** next to the location button. If you want to change your location, tap the location button and make a new selection.

5. Tap within the large text box to enter your post.
6. When you're done entering your post, tap the **Post** button.

Posting a Photo

You can add a photo to any post you make. You can take a new photo for this post, or choose a photo in your phone's library.

Follow these steps:

1. From the Stream screen, tap the **Post** (pencil) button.
2. When the Post screen appears, select your circles and location as previously described.
3. To take a new photo for this post, tap the camera button at the bottom left of the screen. This launches your phone's camera; take a picture and accept it.

   Tap the left button to take a new photo; tap the right button to attach a photo from your library.
4. To attach a photo from your phone's library, tap the library button at the bottom left of the Post screen. When the Photo Albums screen appears, navigate to and select the photo you want to use.
5. A Photo button now appears within the text area of the post screen. Tap the post screen to enter some accompanying text.
6. Tap the **Post** button to post the photo.

Checking In

You don't have to create a full-fledged post to let people know where you are. You can, instead, simply "check in" to a given location; your Google+ friends will then see your location in their streams.

To check into a location, follow these steps:

1. From the home screen, tap the **Stream** icon.
2. When the Stream screen appears, tap the **Checkin** (checkmark) icon at the top right of the screen.
3. When the Checkin At screen appears, as shown in Figure 15.7, tap the location you're at.
4. You now see the post screen; tap the **Post** button to post your location.

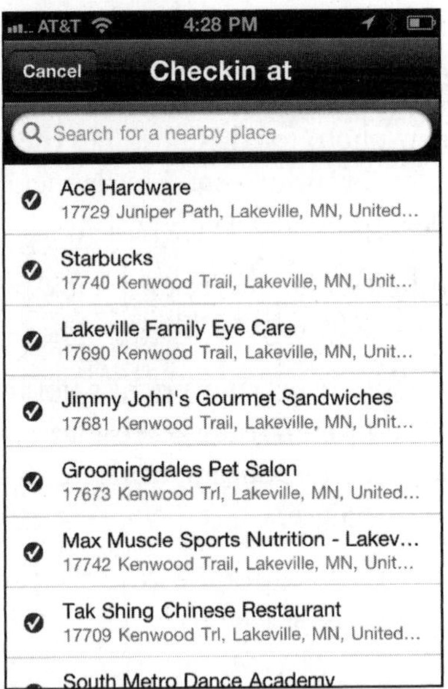

Figure 15.7: *Checking in with Google+.*

GOOGLE+ MINUS

Be cautious about checking in and revealing your location. You may alert some less-than-scrupulous folks (stalkers!) to where you are, physically, or tip off potential burglars that you're not at home.

Viewing and Uploading Photos

The Photos screen in the Google+ app lets you view all the photos you've posted to Google+, as well as photos posted by your friends. To open the Photos screen, shown in Figure 15.8, tap the **Photos** icon on the Home screen.

Figure 15.8: *The Photos screen.*

From here you can do four things:

- Tap **From Your Circles** to view the latest photos from the contacts in your circles.
- Tap **Photos of You** to view any photos in which you're tagged.
- Tap **Your Albums** to view your Google+ photo albums, as shown in Figure 15.9; tap an album to view all the photos within.

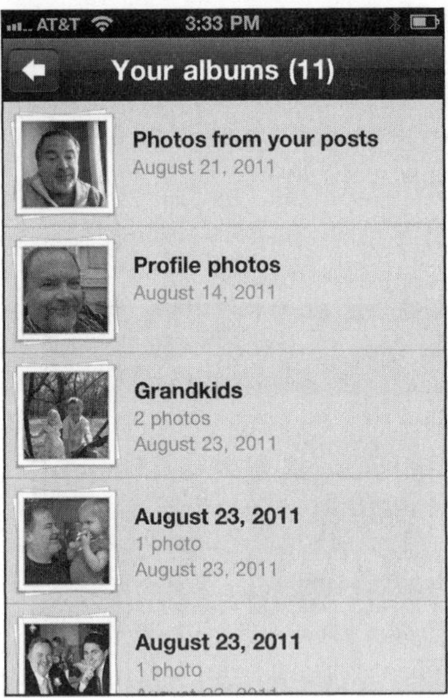

Figure 15.9: *Viewing your photo albums.*

- Tap **From Your Phone** to view photos stored on your phone. (These are photos that have not necessarily been shared with Google+.)

Tap any given photo to view it full-screen on your phone. You can comment on any photo by entering your comments into the text box at the bottom of the photo screen.

Viewing Your Circles and Contacts

When you want to view the people in your circles, or a person's profile page, go to the home screen and tap the **Circles** icon. This displays the Contacts screen. From here you can display your contacts in two different ways:

- Tap the **People** button at the top of the screen to view all your contacts in alphabetical order, as shown in Figure 15.10.
- Tap the **Circles** button at the top of the screen to view your circles. You can then tap a circle to view the people within that circle.

Figure 15.10: *Viewing all your contacts, in alphabetical order.*

When you tap a circle, you view the people you've added to that circle. From this screen you can also view recent posts from these folks, by tapping the **Posts** button at the bottom of the screen. You can also show recently uploaded photos from this circle by tapping the Photos button.

You can also create new circles from your phone. Just go to the circles screen and tap the **New Circle** button at the top right corner. This displays the New Circle screen; enter a name for this circle, then tap the **Create** button.

To view a person's profile, and then add them to a circle, just tap that person's name in the Circles list. This displays the profile screen shown in Figure 15.11. From here you can tap the **About** button to view this person's personal information. Tap the **Posts** button to view this person's most recent posts, or tap the **Photos** button to see photos recently uploaded by this person.

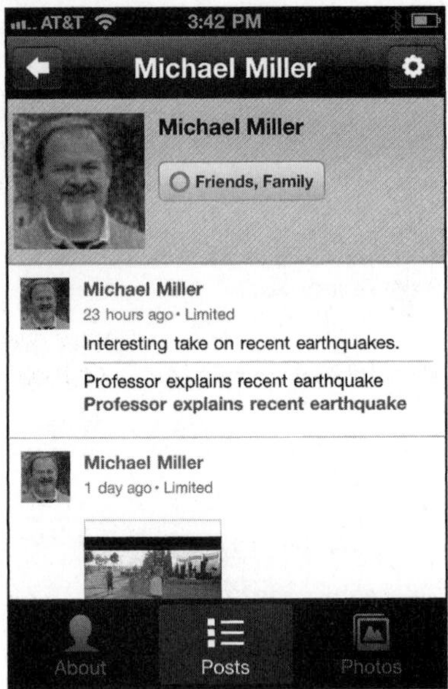

Figure 15.11: *Viewing a profile page.*

To add or change circles for this person, tap the **Circles** button under the person's name. When the Choose Circles screen appears, as shown in Figure 15.12, check the circles you want this person to belong to, then tap the **Done** button.

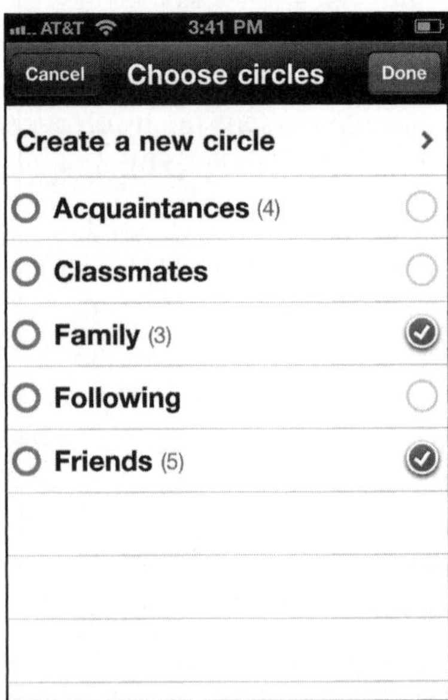

Figure 15.12: *Choosing circles for a contact.*

Viewing Your Profile

Want to view your own profile? Just tap the **Profile** icon on the Google+ home screen. This displays your profile screen. You can then select the **About**, **Posts**, or **Photos** tab.

GOOGLE+ INSIDER

The Google+ mobile app includes a group text chat feature called Messenger. I discuss this in more depth in Chapter 16, so turn there to learn more.

Viewing Notifications

At the bottom of the Google+ home screen is a Notifications area. The number of pending notifications is indicated by red number.

To view your notifications, tap the **Notifications** area. This displays the Notifications screen, shown in Figure 15.13. Tap any notification on this screen to read it in full.

Figure 15.13: *Viewing notifications.*

Configuring Mobile Settings

There are several settings you may want to configure in the Google+ mobile app. You access these settings by tapping the **Settings** (gear) button at the top left of the Home screen.

The Settings screen, shown in Figure 15.14, lets you do the following:

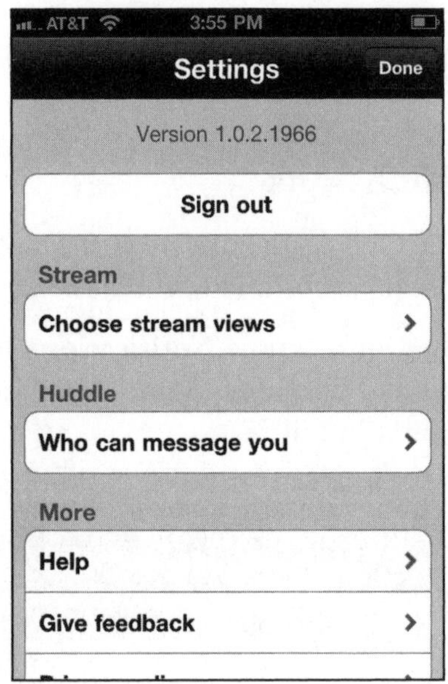

Figure 15.14: *Configuring mobile settings.*

- Sign out of Google+ mobile by tapping **Sign Out**.
- Select circles to view in your Stream by tapping **Choose Stream Views**.
- Select who can text message you by tapping **Who Can Message You**.
- Access Google+'s help system by tapping **Help**.
- Provide feedback to the folks at Google by tapping **Give Feedback**.
- Read Google+'s Privacy Policy by tapping **Privacy Policy**.

- Read Google+'s Terms of Service by tapping **Terms of Service**.

Tap the **Done** button to return to the home screen.

Using the Google+ Mobile Website

If you don't have an iPhone or Android phone, you can access Google+ by using the Google+ mobile website. Just open your phone's web browser and go to m.google.com/plus/.

Viewing the Stream and Making a Post

You now see the mobile stream, shown in Figure 15.15. It functions just like the stream in the Google+ mobile app. Wipe left or right to view streams from different circles.

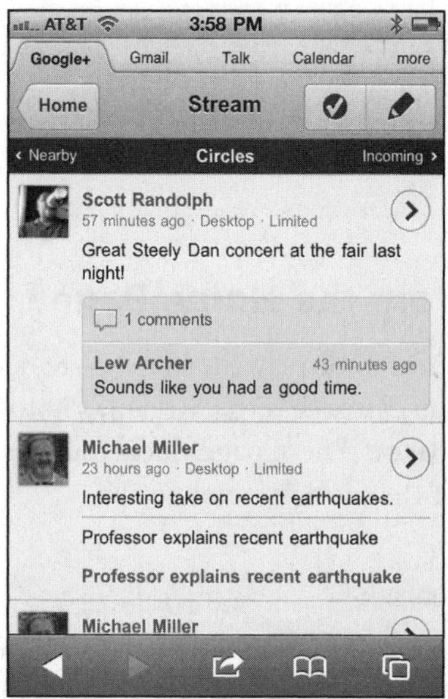

Figure 15.15: *Viewing the stream on the Google+ mobile website.*

To make a new post, tap the **Post** (pencil) button at the top right corner of the screen. This displays the page shown in Figure 15.16. Enter the text of your post into the big text box, select which circles you want to share with, then confirm or change your current location. Tap the **Done** button when you want to post the post.

Figure 15.16: *Making a new post on the mobile website.*

Navigating from the Home Page

Tap the **Home** button to display the home page, shown in Figure 15.17. From here you can access the Stream, Photos, Circles, Profile, and Notifications pages. These pages look and work pretty much like the same screens in the Google+ mobile app.

GOOGLE+ MINUS

At present, the Google+ mobile website does not offer text messaging (Messenger). That could change however, as Google+ evolves, so will the mobile website.

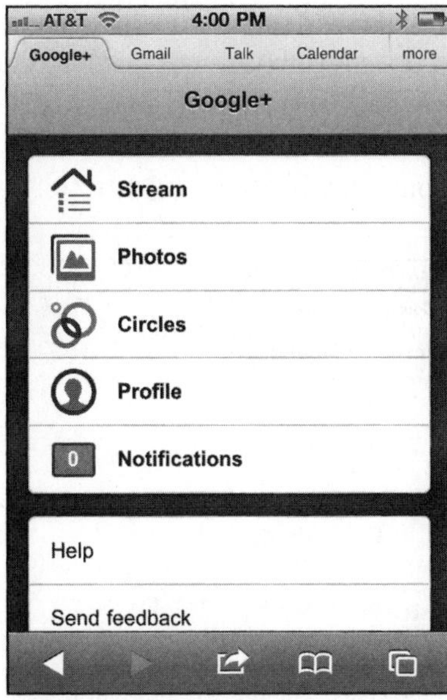

Figure 15.17: *The home page of the Google+ mobile website.*

Figure 15.18, for example, shows the Photos page. From there, you can view photos from your circles, photos of you, and your photo albums.

Figure 15.18: *The Photos page on the mobile website.*

Figure 15.19 shows the circles page. You can view either your circles (tap the **Circles** button) or all your contacts (tap the **People** button). Tap a circle to view everyone within that circle. Tap a person's name to view his or her profile.

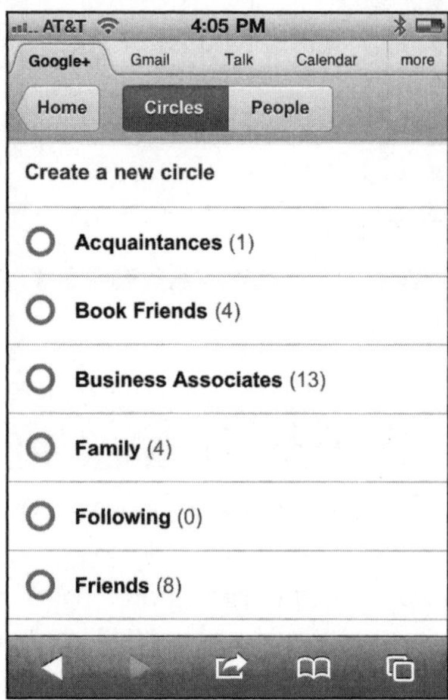

Figure 15.19: *The circles page on the mobile website.*

Figure 15.20 shows a typical profile page. As you can see, you choose from About, Posts, and Photos tabs. Tap the **About** button to view that person's contact information—and contact him via email.

Figure 15.20: *A profile page on the mobile website.*

The Least You Need to Know

- Google+ has mobile apps available for the iPhone and Android phones.
- Other web-enabled phones can access the Google+ mobile website at m.google.com/plus.
- The Home screen of the Google+ mobile app lets you go directly to Stream, Photos, Circles, Messenger (text chat), and your profile.
- You can select which circles you view in your mobile stream—including posts from nearby Google+ users.
- You can post photos you take with your phone or photos from your phone's library.
- You can post your current location by "checking in" with Google+ mobile.

Group Chat with Messenger and Hangouts

Chapter **16**

In This Chapter

- What messenger is and how it works
- Creating a new text chat
- Participating in a conversation
- Controlling who can invite you to a conversation
- Participating in group video chats

In the previous chapter I explained Google+'s mobile versions, in particular the Google+ app available for the iPhone and Android phones. Well, there's one cool new feature that's unique to these mobile apps, and it's well worth your attention.

The feature I'm talking about is called Messenger, and it's a form of mobile group text chat. That's right, we're talking about multi-user instant messaging on your mobile phone. In addition, the Google+ mobile app lets you participate in group video chats, via what G+ calls hangouts.

Text chat or video chat—you make the choice.

Understanding Messenger

By now you know what a text chat is. It's instant messaging—an exchange of text messages between two Google+ users.

What if you wanted to chat with more than just one other friend? That's what Messenger is all about—creating a mobile chat room, called a conversation, that multiple friends can participate in. In fact, up to 50 friends can be part of a conversation.

You can use Messenger for real-time text chatting—that's easy enough to understand. But Messenger can also be used to stay in touch with selected friends when you're on the go. Just create a chat and populate it with the friends you want to keep in touch with. Whenever one of those friends messages you, you'll receive a notification on your mobile phone. You don't have to keep the Google+ app open and live. Google+ pushes the notifications to you.

Creating a Text Chat

How do you create a new text chat? Of course, you must have the Google+ app installed, as explained in the previous chapter. But from there it's really quite easy:

GOOGLE+ INSIDER

The instructions in this chapter cover the Google+ iPhone app. If you're using the Android apps, the operation is very similar.

1. From the Google+ app on your mobile phone, go to the Home screen and tap the **Messenger** icon.
2. When the Messenger screen appears, tap the **Conversation** button in the top right corner, as shown in Figure 16.1.

Figure 16.1: *Tap the* ***Conversation*** *button to create a new conversation.*

3. When the New Conversation page appears, as shown in Figure 16.2, type the names of individuals or circles you want to include.

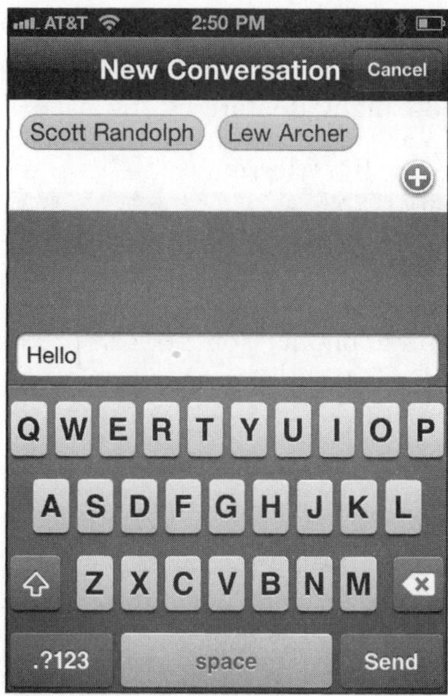

Figure 16.2: *Creating a new conversation.*

4. Enter your initial message or invitation into the Type a Message box.
5. Tap the **Send** button.

Your message is immediately sent to all the people you included in the conversation. They will now receive an invitation to join your conversation.

GOOGLE+ INSIDER

You can have multiple conversations running at the same time.

Participating in a Conversation

You can access all your conversations from the main Messenger screen. You access this screen by tapping the **Messenger** icon from the Google+ mobile home page.

If you've been invited to a conversation, you'll see a number (displayed in red) next to the Messenger icon on the home page. The number indicates how many invitations you have.

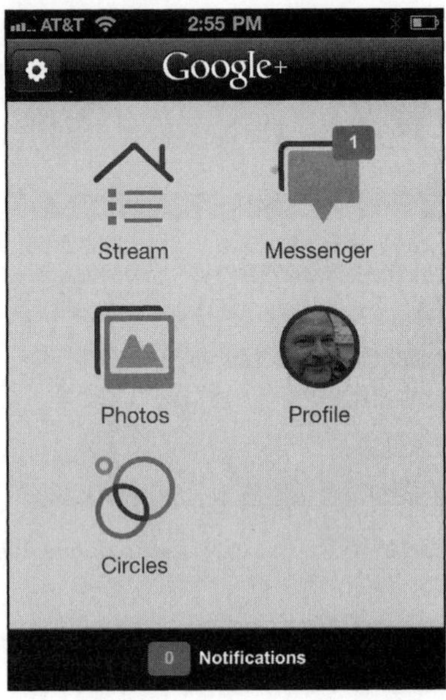

Figure 16.3: *The red number indicates you've been invited to a conversation.*

Joining a Conversation

The Messenger screen itself, shown in Figure 16.4, displays all your open conversations. If you have unread messages in any conversation, you'll see a number off to the right side (displayed in red) indicating how many unread messages there are. To view any specific conversation, just tap it.

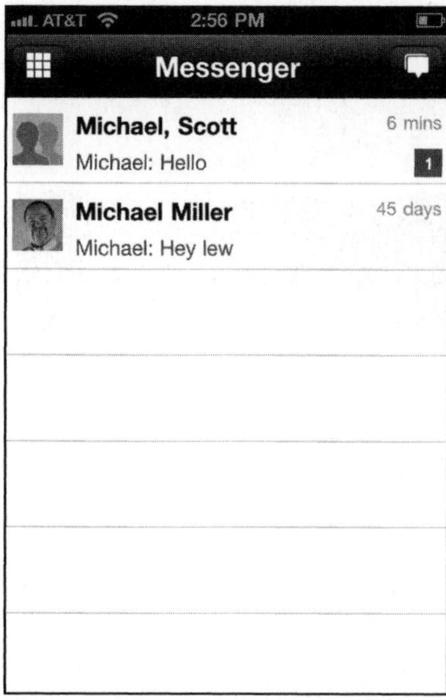

Figure 16.4: *Viewing all your conversations.*

Exchanging Messages

You now see the screen for the selected conversation, like the one shown in Figure 16.5. The profile pictures of conversation members are displayed along the top of the screen. Tap a photo to view that person's profile page.

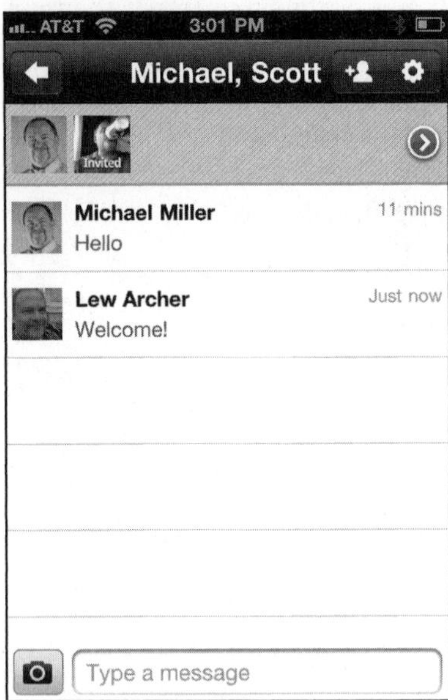

Figure 16.5: *Participating in a conversation.*

The bulk of the screen displays the text of the conversation itself. These messages are displayed in chronological order, with the oldest messages at the top and the newest at the bottom.

To chat with the group, tap the **Type a Message** box at the bottom of the screen. This displays your phone's onscreen keyboard. Next type your message, then tap the **Send** button.

Managing a Conversation

To add someone new to your conversation, tap the **Add Contact** button at the top right of the screen. This displays a list of all your contacts. You then check the person you want to add, then tap the **Done** button. The person will receive an invitation to your conversation.

You can, at any time, leave a conversation. To do this, tap the **Settings** (gear) button in the upper-left corner of the screen to display the Settings page (shown in Figure 16.6), then tap **Leave Conversation**.

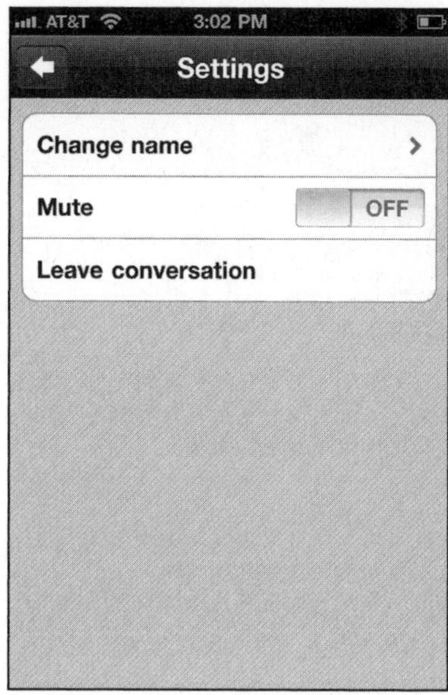

Figure 16.6: *Leaving a conversation.*

Controlling Who Can Message You

You may find that you have certain contacts who want to chat with you more than you want to chat with them. Fortunately, the Google+ mobile app lets you control who can invite you to a conversation.

Follow these steps:

1. From the Google+ mobile home screen, tap the **Settings** (gear) button.
2. When the Settings page appears, as shown in Figure 16.7, go to the Messenger section and tap **Who Can Message You**.

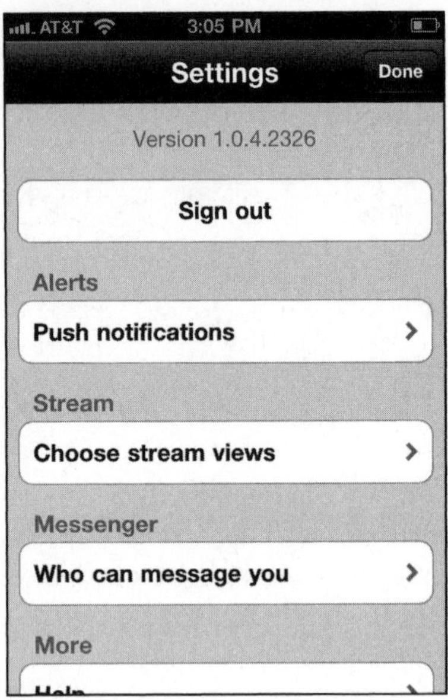

Figure 16.7: *The Settings page.*

3. When the Can Message You screen appears, as shown in Figure 16.8, check one of the following:

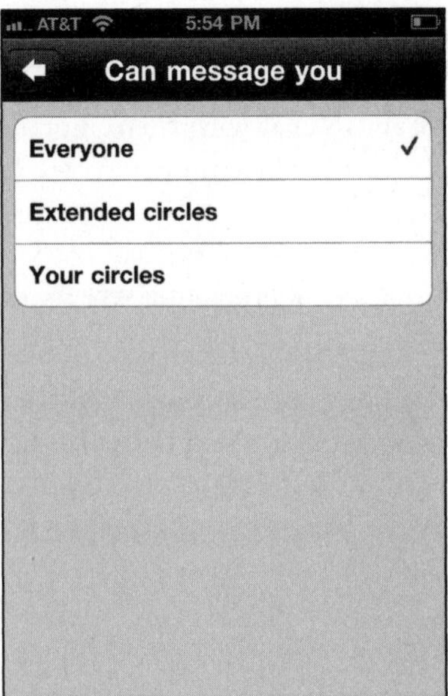

Figure 16.8: *Determining who can invite you to a chat.*

- **Everyone** (any Google+ member)
- **Extended Circles** (people in your circles and people in their circles)
- **Your Circles** (anyone in your circles)

That's it!

Participating in Group Video Hangouts

The Google+ smart phone app also lets you participate in group video chats, or what G+ calls hangouts. (You learned about hangouts in Chapter 11.) All you need is a smart phone with a front-facing camera, and the Google+ app.

You need to be invited to a hangout to participate; you can't initiate hangouts from your phone. But when you receive an invitation to hangout, you see it in your stream. Click the **Join Hangout** button to join the hangout.

When you join a hangout, you see a screen like the one in Figure 16.9. The main participant or presentation appears in a large onscreen window; you appear in a smaller window at the bottom. The thumbnails for other participants in the hangout appear along the top of the screen.

Participating in a hangout is as simple as looking at and talking into your phone as you would with any type of voice chat. To leave a hangout, tap the big **X** at the bottom of the screen.

Figure 16.9: *Participating in a video hangout.*

The Least You Need to Know

- Google+'s mobile app includes the Messenger application, which lets you participate in group text chats called conversations.
- You can invite up to 50 friends in a conversation, and have multiple conversations open at a time.
- If you're getting invited to too many conversations, you can select which people are permitted to invite you.
- You can also participate in group video chats, via Google+ Hangouts.

Doing More with Google+

Part 5

You didn't think we were done yet, did you? From playing to working, Google+'s unique features (including circles and hangouts) allow you to get better connected, be more creative, and get more done than ever before with a single social networking site. What's more, you can add even more functionality to Google+, thanks to some nifty browser extensions.

Read further in this part to learn how to play games on Google+ as well as share your high scores. I'll show you some cool ways to alter your browser and maximize the Google+ experience. And you'll learn to use Google+ with Facebook and Twitter, assuming you want to consolidate things a bit. Finally, I'll show you how to get more creative with circles and hangouts, and even how to use Google+ to market your business. Yowza!

Playing Games

Chapter **17**

In This Chapter

- What social games Google+ offers
- Finding and playing Google+ games
- Sharing game information with friends

Social networking isn't just about talking and sharing. There's also the little matter of playing—games, that is.

If you have a little time on your hands, you'll be glad to know that Google+ lets you play the same type of social games you find on Facebook. Angry Birds and Sudoku, here we come!

Understanding Social Games

The more time you spend on a social network like Google+, the more different things you want to do. Yes, you want to keep tabs on your friends and family, and let them know what you're up to. You also want to share some photos and videos, and maybe even do a little real-time chatting.

But all talk and no play makes Jack and Jill dull kids. Recognizing this, Google+ has added a Games section, so that you can while away the spare moments playing a game or two.

The games you find on Google+ are what we call social games—games with some sort of social element to them. This typically involves pitting yourself against other Google Plusers online, or sharing your game accomplishments with your circles of friends.

Let's review that last statement. Google+ will share the games you play and information about those games with other Google+ users. That typically means sharing your high scores, levels achieved, and other accomplishments with friends and other game players. It's all part and parcel of making social connections—in this instance, through social game play.

What kinds of games are available? As I write this, Google+'s games section has just been launched, so the selection isn't quite as broad as what you're likely to find by the time this book is published. But at launch, here are the games that were available:

- Angry Birds
- Bejeweled Blitz
- Bubble Island
- City of Wonder
- CityVille
- Collapse! Blast
- Crime City
- Diamond Dash
- Dragon Age Legends
- Dragons of Atlantis
- Edgeworld
- Flood-It!
- Global Warfare
- Monster World
- Sudoku Puzzles
- Wild Ones
- Zombie Lane
- Zynga Poker

I think it's likely that Google+ will quickly attract the attention of all the major social games developers—which means we'll see popular games like FarmVille and Mafia Wars making their way from Facebook to Google+. Trust me on this one—Google+ games will be a big thing.

GOOGLE+ INSIDER

Games are an enormous money-maker for any social network. Facebook, for example, generated approximately $400 million in game revenue in 2010. It does this by taking a 30% cut of all revenues generated by the games on its site, as well as selling advertising to those same game companies. (Many games let players buy in-game items or currency, for real money.) Google is trying to attract game developers to Google+ by only taking 5% of game revenues. This should jumpstart Google+'s games section, while still generating a hefty amount of revenue for Google.

Finding Games in Google+

Where are all the games in Google+? On the Games page, of course. You get there by clicking the **Games** button at the top of any Google+ page (see Figure 17.1). The default tab, Featured Games, displays those games that Google+ is pushing at the moment. Click the **All Games** tab to view all available games, as shown in Figure 17.2.

GOOGLE+ INSIDER

There's a third tab on the Games page, labeled Game Notifications. All the information shared by Google+ games, as well as invitations and other notices, are found here. Any unread notifications are indicated by a number next to the tab name; click the tab to view all such notifications.

Figure 17.1: *Google+'s featured games.*

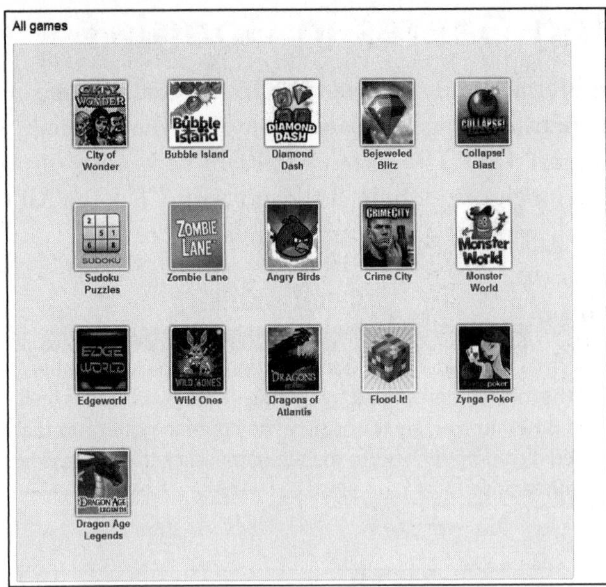

Figure 17.2: *Viewing all of Google+'s games.*

Playing a Game

Now that you know how to find Google+ Games, how do you play them? It's really quite easy.

To play a game, follow these steps:

1. Click the **Games** button at the top of any Google+ page.
2. When the Games page appears, hover over the game you want to play and click the **Play** button.
3. The first time you play a game, you may see a permissions window. Click in the affirmative to continue.

The game now loads in your browser window, as shown in Figure 17.3. Each game is different, of course, so you'll need to read the instructions to figure out what to do next.

Figure 17.3: *Playing Flood-It!.*

To exit a game, click one of the Google+ Navigation buttons at the top of the page.

Sharing Game Information

What you can share with your friends depends on the specific game. For example, when you enter the Bejeweled Blitz game you see an Invite Friends button. Click this button and you see the Select People pane, shown in Figure 17.4. Select which of your friends you want to invite to play with you, then click the **Preview** button. Google+ now displays a preview of the invitation; click the **Send** button to send the invite on its way.

Figure 17.4: *Inviting friends to play a game.*

Your friends receive an invitation like the one shown in Figure 17.5. They can then join the fun by clicking the **Play Now** link.

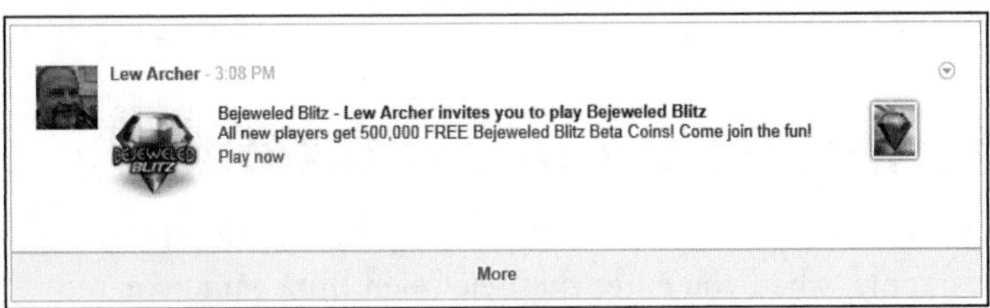

Figure 17.5: *A typical Google+ game invitation.*

As another example, when multiple friends are playing Bejeweled Blitz, all their names and statistics appear on the leader board, as shown in Figure 17.6. This way you can keep track of how your friends are doing.

Figure 17.6: *Viewing your friends' game statistics.*

And, if you generate a high score, the game will prompt you to share it with your friends. If you opt to do this, you'll see the Share pane shown in Figure 17.7. Select which friends or circles you want to share with, then click the **Share** button.

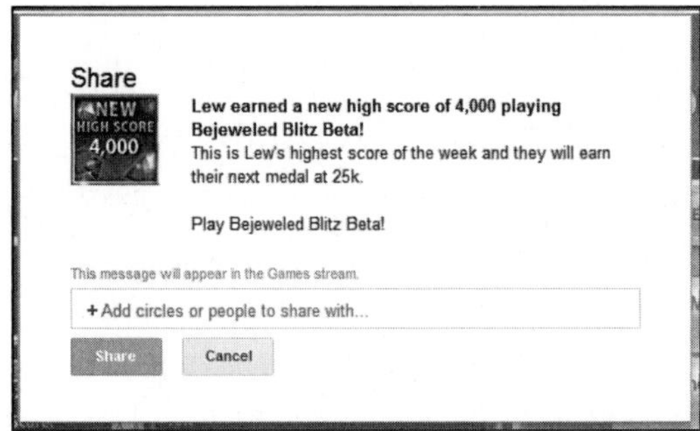

Figure 17.7: *Sharing a high score with friends.*

As I said, each game is going to work its own way and offer its own sharing options. Rest assured, these are all social games, so you should be able to share a lot with your Google+ friends.

The Least You Need to Know

- Google+ offers a variety of social games you can play with your friends.
- All games are located on the Games page; click a game to start playing.
- You can invite friends to play with you, or choose to share your game information with friends.

Extending Google+

Chapter

18

In This Chapter

- What a Chrome extension is and does
- Downloading and installing extensions in your Chrome browser
- Finding the best extensions and applications for Google+

If you're using the Google Chrome web browser, you can add some useful functionality by installing extensions to the browser. These are add-in programs that let the browser perform specific operations that it couldn't previously.

As this is a book about Google+, it's worth looking at those Chrome extensions that offer Google+ functionality. It's a great way to get more use out of Google+, from within the Chrome browser.

Understanding Chrome Extensions

You browse the web using a web browser. There are many browsers out there, including Microsoft's Internet Explorer, Mozilla Firefox, and Google Chrome.

For our purposes, Chrome is the most interesting of the bunch, as it's developed by Google—the same folks behind Google+. As you might suspect, there are some synergies to be had when using Google Chrome to access Google+.

GOOGLE+ INSIDER

The extensions discussed in this chapter work only with the Google Chrome web browser. They do not work with Internet Explorer or Firefox. If you're not yet using Google Chrome, you can download it for free from www.google.com/chrome.

These synergies come in the form of browser extensions. These are add-in programs that install directly into the Chrome browser, and add increased functionality. As you might suspect, there are a ton of Chrome extensions specifically for Google+.

For example, you can find Chrome extensions that let you +1 any web page, add your Google+ posts to your Twitter feed, zoom into Google+ photos, and more. And here's the great thing—all these extensions (as well as thousands of other non-Google+ extensions) are all free.

Downloading and Installing Extensions

Where do you find these Chrome extensions? In Google's Chrome Web Store, of course. Just go to chrome.google.com/webstore/ and look for the Extensions pane in the left column, as shown in Figure 18.1. From there, you can browse available extensions by category, or use the top-of-page search box to search for specific extensions by keyword.

Extensions are organized in the Chrome Web Store by category—Accessibility, Blogging, Developer Tools, Fun, News & Weather, Photos, Productivity, Search Tools, Shopping, Social & Communications, Sports, and those extensions developed by Google. Since Google+ extensions bridge several categories, they're best found by searching for **"Google+"** (in quotation marks) or the extension name.

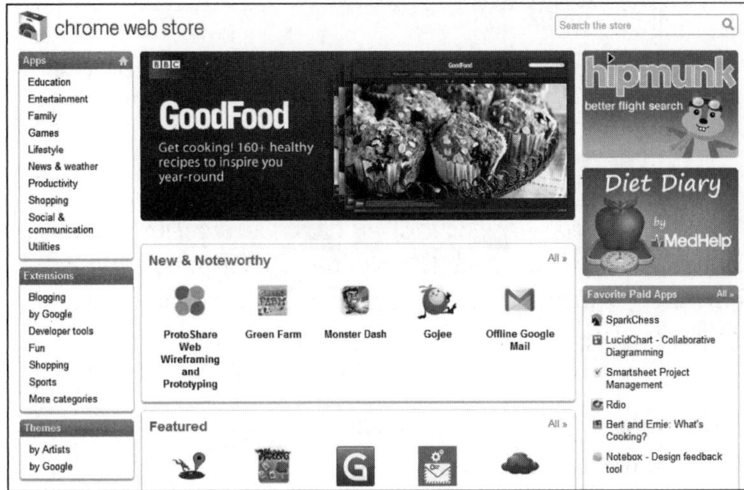

Figure 18.1: *The Chrome Web Store.*

Here's how to find and download an extension:

1. From within the Chrome browser, go to chrome.google.com/webstore/.

2. Enter the name of the extension or **google+** into the search box at the top of the page, then press **Enter**.

3. Google now displays all extensions, apps, and themes that match your query, as shown in Figure 18.2. Since we're interested specifically in extensions, scroll to the Search Results in Extensions section and click the **All** link.

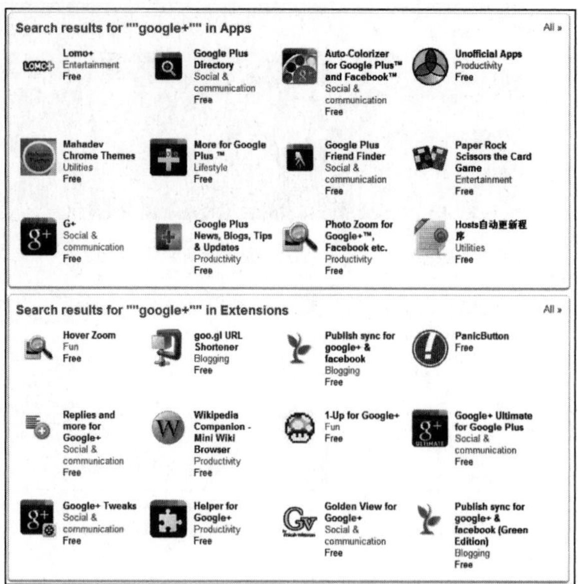

Figure 18.2: *The results of a Chrome Web Store search.*

4. You now see all extensions that match your query. Click an extension to learn more about that item.

5. Google now displays the page for the selected extension, like the one in Figure 18.3. Read about the extension, then click the **Add to Chrome** button if you decide to install.

6. If you are prompted to confirm the installation, click the **Install** button.

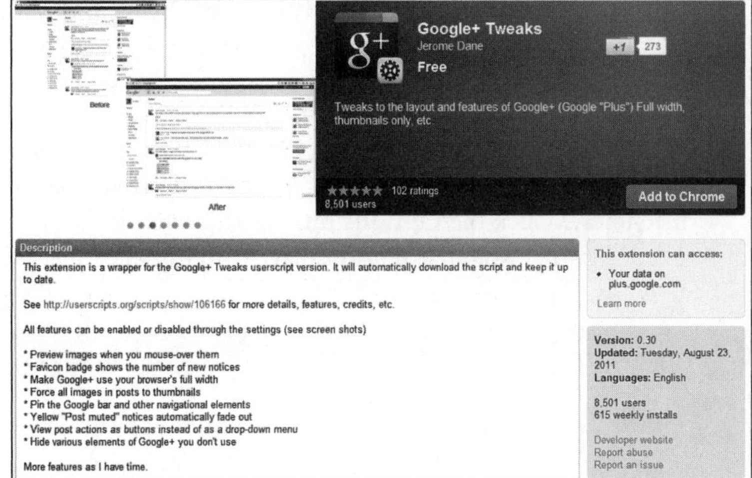

Figure 18.3: *Viewing the page for a Chrome extension.*

Most Chrome extensions add some sort of button to the Chrome toolbar. You activate the extension by clicking this button.

GOOGLE+ INSIDER

While some Chrome extensions are developed by Google, most come from third-party developers.

Managing Extensions

Given the extensions discussed in this chapter, it's easy to go a little crazy and completely clutter your toolbar with bounteous buttons. Fortunately, it's easy enough to manage the extensions you've downloaded and installed. You can configure extension options, temporarily disable extensions, and permanently uninstall those extensions you no longer want.

Configuring Extension Options

Some extensions need to be configured for your personal use. To configure an extension, follow these steps.

1. Click the **Customize and Control** (wrench) button in the Chrome toolbar.
2. Select **Tools > Extensions**.
3. This opens the Extensions tab in Google Chrome. As you can see in Figure 18.4, all the extensions you've downloaded are listed here. Click the **Options** link for the extension you wish to configure. (Not all extensions have configurable options.)

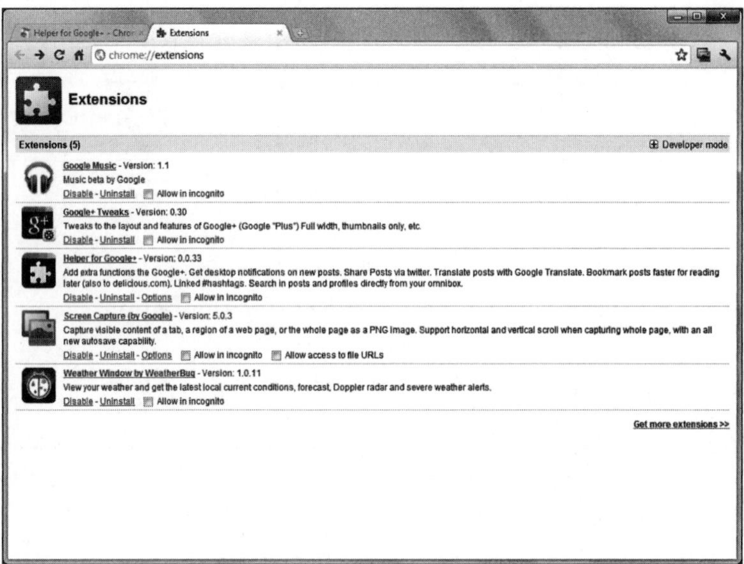

Figure 18.4: *Managing installed extensions.*

4. When the extension's configuration page appears in a new tab, select the appropriate settings, then close the tab. (Figure 18.5 shows a typical configuration page.)

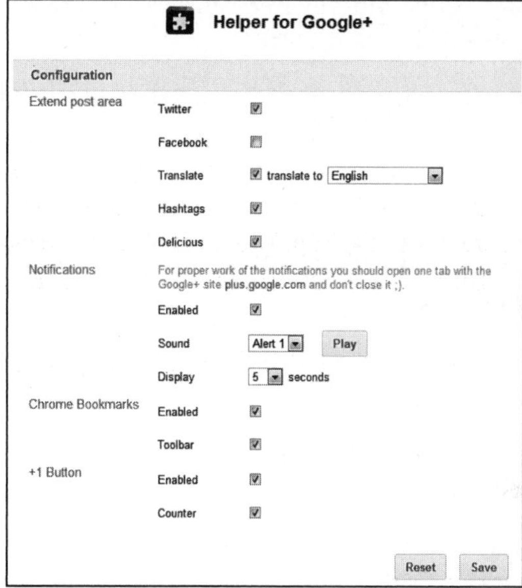

Figure 18.5: *Configuring a Chrome extension.*

Disabling or Uninstalling Extensions

If you find you're not actively using a given extension, you can disable it within Google Chrome. If you think you'll never use a given extension again, the better choice is to completely uninstall it.

Here's how to do both:

1. Click the **Customize and Control** (wrench) button on the Google Chrome toolbar.
2. Select **Tools** > **Extensions**.
3. This opens the Extensions tab. To disable an extension, click the **Disable** link for that item.

GOOGLE+ PLUS

You can later enable any extension you've disabled by returning to the Extensions tab and clicking **Enable** for that extension.

4. To completely uninstall an extension, click that item's **Uninstall** link.
5. When asked to confirm the uninstallation, click the **Uninstall** button.

Discovering Google+ Extensions for Chrome

So what cool extensions can you find for Google+? Here's a list of some of the more popular ones:

+1 Button. Lets you +1 any web page you visit, from a new +1 button added to the Chrome Address box.

+Everything. Adds the Google navigation bar to all websites, not just Google sites.

+Photo Zoom. Lets you zoom into any photo in your Stream by hovering over it.

-1 Minus One. Adds a -1 button to all Google+ posts; click the -1 button to "dislike" a post.

Beautify G+. Fixes the position of the menu bar, left column, and right column; lets you +1 any web page you visit; enables audio notifications; and more.

Everything Went Black for Google Plus. Enables a sticky or floating header bar and replaces the normal Google+ logo with a black one.

Extended Share for Google Plus. Adds a "Share On" link to all your Google+ posts, which lets you easily share each post with Facebook, Twitter, LinkedIn, and other social networks.

G+me for Google Plus. Makes large Google+ Streams easier to use, by collapsing posts, hiding comments, and the like.

Gmail for Google Plus. Integrates your Gmail account into your Google+ page.

Golden View for Google+. Lets you mute posts from specific users, set a default circle, hide images and comments, and search Google+ from within Google search.

Google+ Tweaks. Lets you tweak the Google+ layout. For example, you can force all images in posts to thumbnails, preview images on mouseover, stretch Google+ to the full width of your browser, pin the Google navigation bar, and hide aspects of Google+ you don't use.

Google+ Ultimate. Lets you change the Google+ theme, enables floating top and left navigation, resizes images to thumbnails, and more.

Helper for Google+. Adds a variety of extra functions to Google+; lets you share Google+ posts on Twitter, translate foreign-language posts, get notification of new posts on your desktop, bookmark posts for later viewing, and more.

Layouts for Google Plus. Lets you change the Google+ background image.

Move Your Photos. Helps you transfer your Facebook photos to Picasa Web Albums for viewing within Google+.

My Hangouts for Google Plus. Displays all your active Hangouts in your Google+ Stream.

Notification Count for Google Plus. Displays a count of unread Google+ notifications in the Google Chrome toolbar, right next to the Address box.

Publish Sync for Google+ & Facebook. Synchronizes all your posts to Google+, Facebook, Twitter, and other social networking sites.

Replies and More for Google Plus. Adds Reply and Reply to Author options to all Google+ posts, so you can more easily mention people in your comments without using the + or @ signs.

Search Extension for Google Plus. Lets you search Google+ public posts and profiles.

SGPlus. Automatically posts to Facebook, Twitter, and LinkedIn whenever you make a post to Google+; also displays your Facebook, Twitter, and LinkedIn feeds within your Google+ Stream.

Share+ Social Buttons for Google Plus. Lets you share Google+ posts with other social media sites.

Surplus. Adds an icon to the Chrome toolbar that lets you display a notification bubble—and then respond within the bubble.

Tweets +1. Adds Google's +1 button to your Twitter page, so that you can +1 tweets directly from Twitter.

Usability Boost for Google Plus. Changes the overall Google+ design to improve readability.

Discovering Useful Google+ Apps

The Chrome Web Store also includes several applications (apps) that add functionality to Google+. You can find and download these apps the same way you find and download Chrome extensions; the difference is, an app runs in its own web page, like a regular software application.

Here are some of the more useful Google+-related apps:

Auto-Colorizer for Google Plus and Facebook. Lets you change Google+'s color scheme. (Also works with Facebook to do the same thing.)

Google Plus Directory. A searchable directory of Google+ users.

Google Plus Friend Finder. Searchable directory of Google+ users; lets you find friends by city, country, occupation, and more.

Google Plus Mania. Displays the latest news and blog posts about Google+.

More for Google Plus. Automatically loads more content as you scroll to the bottom of the Google+ Stream.

Photo Zoom for Google+. Enlarges thumbnails when you mouse-over the image.

The Least You Need to Know

- An extension is a plug-in that extends the functionality of Google's Chrome web browser.
- An app is a small web-based application.
- The Chrome Web Store contains numerous extensions and apps that make Google+ easier to use.

Using Google+ with Other Social Networks

Chapter

19

In This Chapter

- Transferring your Facebook data to Google+
- Posting from Google+ to Facebook and Twitter
- Reading Facebook and Twitter posts in your Google+ Stream
- Deciding to integrate your Google+ account with other social networks

There's a good chance that Google+ isn't the first or only social network you've used. And even if you don't use them yourself, you probably have a fair number of friends, family members, and colleagues who use Facebook, Twitter, LinkedIn, and other social media.

Since some degree of cross pollination is inevitable, there is value in learning how to use Google+ with these other social networks. If nothing else, you need to minimize the amount of time you spend posting to and reading posts from all the different social networks.

Transferring Facebook Data to Google+

Let's start with those of you who are already Facebook members. If you've used Facebook at all, you have a fair amount of time and information invested in Facebook, and you probably don't want to abandon it. Wouldn't it be nice if there were some way to get your personal information, contacts, and photographs from Facebook to Google+?

Well, there is—although it isn't always easy. Let me tell you about it.

Exporting Your Facebook Data

I'll start with the raw data you've personally added to Facebook—in particular, your digital photos and videos. These can be moved to Google+ with surprising ease.

The way you do this is to download all this information from Facebook into a file. You then upload this file to Google+.

Here's how it works:

1. Log in to your Facebook account, click the **Account** button in the navigation bar, and select **Account Settings**.
2. When Facebook's Account Settings page appears, as shown in Figure 19.1, select the **General** tab and click the **Download a Copy of Your Facebook Data** link.

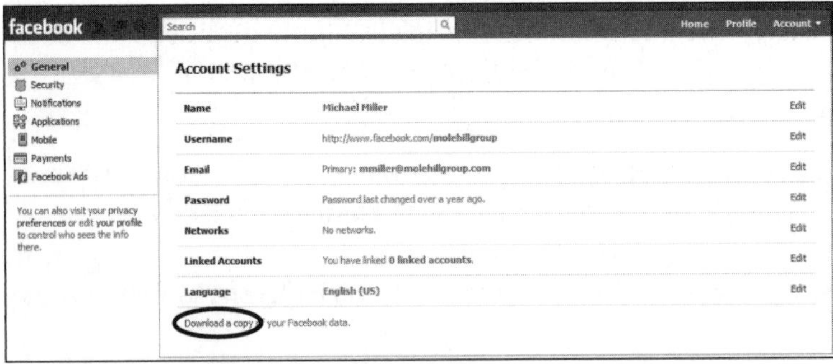

Figure 19.1: *Getting ready to download your data from Facebook.*

3. When the Download Your Information page appears, click the **Start My Archive** button.
4. When the Request My Download dialog box appears, click the **Start My Archive** button.

5. Facebook assembles all the data and photos, and sends you an email when the file is ready. Click the link in the email message.

GOOGLE+ INSIDER

It may take several minutes to an hour for Facebook to create your download file and notify you that it's ready.

6. You're now taken to a different Download Your Information page on the Facebook site, as shown in Figure 19.2. Enter your password, as requested, then click the **Continue** button.

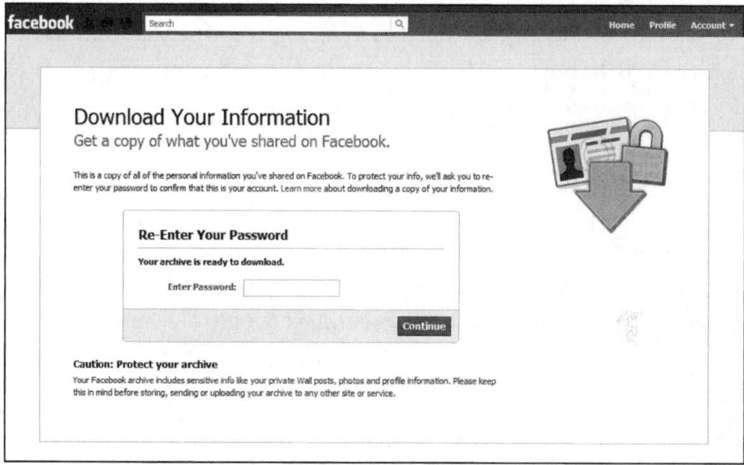

Figure 19.2: *Downloading your Facebook data.*

7. When the next page appears, click the **Download Archive** button.

8. When prompted, save this file to the desired location on your computer's hard drive. The file should be in compressed (zip) format.

9. Extract (unzip) the file you downloaded.

The extracted data should be organized into multiple folders, labeled HTML, Photos, and Videos. Launch the extracted index.html file to view your profile, messages, and other content.

Importing Photos and Videos into Google+

Once your Facebook data is downloaded to your computer, you can then upload that same data to Google+. Now, you can't import everything; in particular, you cannot import your Facebook profile information or status updates and messages. (You probably wouldn't want to send old Facebook messages to your new Google+ friends, anyway.) You can, however, import your photos and videos, which is a big thing.

To import your Facebook photos into Google+, go to Google+ and click the **Photos** button. When the Photos page appears, click the **Upload New Photos** button, select the photos in your Facebook Photos folder, and upload them.

To import your Facebook videos into Google+, go to Google+ and click the **Profile** button. When your Profile page appears, select the **Videos** tab, and click the **Upload New Videos** button. Next, select the videos in your Facebook Videos folder and upload them.

Importing Facebook Friends

Even though Facebook exports your Facebook friends data, there's no good way to import those friends into Google+. The better approach is to ignore the data you downloaded and simply link your Facebook account with a Yahoo! Mail account. (Yahoo! has a good working relationship with Facebook; Google doesn't.) You can then connect your Yahoo! Mail contacts with Google+.

To perform this procedure, you must have a Google+ account (of course), a Facebook account, and a Yahoo! Mail account. You start by exporting your Facebook contacts into Yahoo! Mail, by following these steps:

1. Sign in to your Yahoo! Mail account (mail.yahoo.com) and click the **Contacts** tab.
2. From the Contacts tab, click the **Import Contacts** button.
3. When the Import Contacts page appears, click the **Facebook** icon.

4. When the Share with Yahoo! dialog box appears, click the **Okay** button.

Yahoo! now imports your Facebook friends as new email contacts and notifies you when done. Now you get to import those same contacts into Google+. Follow these steps:

1. Sign in to Google+ (plus.google.com) and click the **Circles** button at the top of the page.
2. When the Circles page appears, click the **Find People** tab.
3. In the Find Friends section, click the **Yahoo!** link.
4. When the Yahoo! window opens, make sure the correct Yahoo! email account is selected, then click the **Agree** button.
5. Google+ now imports your Yahoo! contacts (which include your Facebook contacts) and displays them on your Circles page.

Since a Google+ friend isn't really a friend until he's added to a circle, you now need to add your Facebook friends to your circles; to do so, just drag a contact onto the desired circle. If any of your Facebook friends are not yet members of Google+, they'll receive an email invitation to join up.

Posting to Facebook, Twitter, etc. from Google+

Importing your Facebook data to Google+ is a one-time thing. What you'll deal with on a daily basis, however, is posting to Google+, Facebook, and other social networks.

Do you have to make separate posts to each social network? Fortunately, no. There are several browser extensions and add-ins that let you create one post and send it to multiple social networks.

Several of these extensions were covered in Chapter 18. Some of these are available for browsers other than Google Chrome. Read on to learn more.

GOOGLE+ INSIDER

There are several programs, such as HootSuite (www.hootsuite.com) and TweetDeck (www.tweetdeck.com), that integrate reading and posting between Facebook and Twitter. At this date these programs do not include Google+ integration. It is possible, however, that these programs will be updated to include Google+ functionality. Check with the respective developers for more information.

G++ for Google Plus

G++ for Google Plus is a browser extension for Google Chrome and Firefox—it is not available for Internet Explorer. This extension lets you read Facebook and Twitter feeds in your Google+ Stream, as well as post Facebook and Twitter updates directly from Google+.

Google+Facebook

Google+Facebook is a browser extension for Google Chrome, Internet Explorer, and Firefox that integrates your Facebook and Google+ accounts. When installed, you see a Facebook button in the Google+ navigation bar; click this button to view your Facebook News Feed as a Google+ Stream.

This extension does not let you cross-post to both Facebook and Google+. It's only for viewing Facebook posts in Google+, but still fairly useful. Learn more and download the free extension at www.crossrider.com/install/519-google-facebook.

Google+Tweet

Google+Tweet, developed by the same folks behind Google+Facebook, is a browser extension for Google Chrome, Internet Explorer, and Firefox. It integrates your Twitter account into Google+.

When installed, Google+Tweet lets you create a single message and post it to both Google+ and Twitter. (The message has to be 140 characters or less, of course, to tweet properly.) It also lets you view your Twitter feed from within your Google+ Stream.

Learn more and download the free extension at www.crossrider.com/install/529-google-tweet.

Publish Sync for Google+ & Facebook

This extension is only available for Google Chrome. It lets you post from Google+ to both Facebook and Twitter, and vice versa. (It does not integrate the reading of news feeds, however.) You can find this free extension in the Chrome Web Store.

SGPlus

SGPlus is a browser extension for Google Chrome, Internet Explorer, and Firefox that lets you view your Facebook, Twitter, LinkedIn, and RSS feeds from within Google+. You can also use SGPlus to automatically post your Google+ posts to Facebook, Twitter, and LinkedIn.

This extension also lets you import your Facebook photos into Google+. Learn more and download this free extension at www.sgplus.me.

Posting from Google+ to Other Social Networks via Email

You don't have to install a browser extension to post from Google+ to other social networks. If your social network lets you post via email (both Facebook and Twitter do), you can send Google+ posts to an email address and thus cross-post to the other network. First, I'll explain how this works with Facebook and then Twitter.

Posting via Email to Facebook

You start by going to www.facebook.com/mobile/, then scrolling to the Upload via Email section. Click the **Send My Upload Email to Me Now** link to receive your personal upload email address. Write it down.

This email address needs to be added to your Google+ Circles, as if it were just another contact. From within Google+, click the **Circles** button and add your Facebook upload email address to one or more of your circles.

GOOGLE+ PLUS

You may want to create a new circle just for posting to Facebook and Twitter.

Now, whenever you post from Google+, include this circle or email address in your sharing. Make sure you click the **Also Email Person Not Yet Using Google+** link, when prompted.

Your post will now be sent via email to Facebook, and then posted as a Facebook status update. Voila!

Posting via Email to Twitter

The email posting process works pretty much the same with Twitter. You start by going to tweetymail (www.tweetymail.com), a service that lets you tweet via email. Sign up for an account to receive your personal email posting address.

With that email address in hand, return to Google+ and add the address to one or more circles. When you next post from Google+, include this circle or email address in your sharing. Make sure you click the **Also Email Person Not Yet Using Google+** link, and your post will now be sent via email to tweetymail and then tweeted for all your Twitter followers to read.

Don't Use Google+ with Other Social Networks

So far in this chapter I've assumed that if you have accounts at multiple social networks, you want to integrate them for easier use. But maybe you don't.

There are a number of reasons why you might want to keep your Google+, Facebook, Twitter, and LinkedIn accounts separate. I'll work through some of the major ones here.

Different Rules Apply

Every social network is different. The acceptable posting frequency, as well as the content of your posts, differs from one network to another.

For example, Twitter users are expected to tweet several times a day. If you do that on Facebook or Google+, you may overload your readers; posting once a day or so is probably better. And posting once a week is probably adequate for LinkedIn.

Then there's the matter of post length. Twitter is the bottleneck here, since tweets can be no more than 140 characters in length. On Facebook, however, you can post up to 5,000 characters, and Google+'s character limit is ... well, pretty much as long as you want. If you try to post universally, you'll either artificially limit your Google+ (and possibly Facebook) posts, or end up writing way more than can be included in a tweet. This is one instance where one size definitely does not fit all.

The contents of your posts may vary from network to network, as well. Perhaps due to Twitter's length restrictions, tweets tend to be more direct and less detailed than what you find on Facebook and Google+. The latter two networks allow and seemingly encourage more in-depth information and personal reflections—although Google+ users, at least in these early days, seems to shy away from the more intimate whining that unfortunately plagues Facebook.

The point is, each social network has its own community personality, and trying to post the same messages to each ignore this fact. It may be convenient to synchronize your posting, but you run the risk of sounding a bit out of synch with each individual network.

You Need to Participate in Each Community Separately

Speaking of community personality, you won't get much of a flavor of it if you don't actually visit the sites in question. Consolidating all your friends' posts from multiple sites is definitely a timesaver, but by reading posts in this fashion you miss all the context.

Look, if you want to play the game you have to get down on the court; you can't do it by remote control. There's a certain zeitgeist you experience when scrolling through your Google+ Stream or browsing your Facebook News Feed, and you miss all that if you read the posts on another site. I'm not saying you can't or shouldn't do it this way, but if you really want to become immersed in the community, you have to visit there.

You Might Look Like a Spammer

Here's another danger of sending the same posts to multiple sites—you run the danger of looking like a spammer. This is especially true to those who have accounts on all the sites; they'll see your same exact message multiple times.

Here's a real-world example. My son-in-law is an active tweeter and Facebooker. (He hasn't moved to Google+ yet, but he probably will soon.) He uses a third-party solution to post his tweets to Facebook, because that's more efficient. The problem is, if you read your Twitter feed and then read your Facebook News Feed, you see the same posts twice. Sometimes it's worse, because he forgets and makes the same post manually to both sites, which then gets duplicated again by the syncing service. It's particularly noticeable when I use a posting consolidation service myself, so I see all his tweets and status updates lined up in a row. It definitely looks like spam.

Now, you might not care if you look like a spammer. That's fine. But it's a big potential problem for businesses that use posting software or services to write once and post to multiple sites. Just something to keep in mind.

Google+ Is a Chance to Start Over

Here's the final reason why you might want to keep Google+ separate from your other social network accounts. For many folks, Google+ represents a chance to start over in the social networking world, and bringing their old contacts along for the ride defeats that purpose.

You see, there's a whole group of people who are burned out on Facebook (especially), Twitter, and other current social networks. They have hundreds of Facebook friends and they get inundated with tweets and status updates from people they don't know and don't care about. They've felt obligated to "friend" strangers and acquaintances who aren't really friends, and feel strangled by the chaotic forced social interactions.

For these folks (and you may be one of them), Google+ is the opportunity to abandon the past and start fresh. With the circles feature, it lets them start assembling and organizing social connections in a logical fashion. (You really can't organize hundreds of Facebook friends once you have them.) It's a new beginning, readily achievable by abandoning the past.

So if you view Google+ as a new beginning, you might resist the temptation to connect back up with all of the same Facebook and Twitter friends. Accept Google+ as the new reality, and have fun living within it.

The Least You Need to Know

- Facebook lets you download a master data file which you can use to import your profile information, photos, and videos into Google+.
- There are several browser extensions available that let you post from Google+ to Facebook and Twitter, and to read your Facebook and Twitter feeds in your Google+ Stream.
- You may not want to integrate your Google+ account with other social networks, however; each network has its own posting rules and community characteristics which may not be compatible.

More Creative Uses for Circles

Chapter **20**

In This Chapter

- Strategies for managing Google+ Circles
- Organizing your contacts into different types of circles
- Using empty circles to store your favorite posts

Google+'s most distinguishing feature is the ability to organize your friends into circles—and then use those circles to filter the posts you make and receive. If you put your mind to it, there's a lot you can do with these circles—all in the name of making Google+ both more efficient and more effective for you to use.

How Should You Approach Circles?

Among folks who have been using Google+ for a while, the same question seems to inevitably arise. What is your circle strategy? That is, how do you approach the naming and organization of Google+ Circles?

The first thing you need to decide is whether you want to create a lot of very specific circles, or just a handful of general circles. There are pros and cons for each approach.

GOOGLE+ PLUS

Remember that you can add people to multiple circles; it's not just one circle per person. For example, some co-workers might also be friends. (Or not; depends on the co-worker.)

Embracing the Two Circle Strategy

If you want to simplify your life, start by simplifying your social networking. The easiest way to do this is to create just two circles—Friends and Everybody Else. You put your closest friends—the people you really want to communicate with—into the Friends circle, and you put everybody else into the Everybody Else circle.

The benefits to this approach are that it's simple; it requires less work (fewer circles to create and manage); and it requires less thinking (either someone's a real friend or they're not). As to that less work thing, you'll want to read posts from the Friends circle daily, but you can probably put off reading posts from Everybody Else until later in the week—or just ignore them completely.

It's not a very refined strategy; we're talking kind of a brute force approach to social segmentation. But it does boil everything down to the essentials.

Embracing Google+'s Default Circle Strategy

If cutting down to just two circles is too draconian for you, then you may just want to accept Google+'s default circles. This way you don't have to create any new circles or give a whole lot of thought as to how you want to organize things; you accept Google's judgment and work from there.

Who should go into these four circles? Here's what I recommend:

Friends. Your closest friends—the people you actually communicate with on a regular basis. These folks will probably see the bulk of your posts.

Family. Family members only—both immediate and extended. You'll want to keep people in this circle informed of typical family matters.

Acquaintances. So-called Facebook friends—people you feel obligated to follow, to some degree, but with whom you'll probably never communicate face-to-face. You'll end up not posting a lot to these folks.

Following. Celebrities, performers, politicians, and businesses that you want to read posts from, but probably will never post to.

Embracing the Multiple Circle Strategy

If your life is even somewhat complex, you probably can't divide your relationships into just four buckets. You need to granulize the way you think of relationships, fine-tuning the way you group your friends, family, and colleagues. That means creating a lot of different circles, each targeted at a very specific group of people or type of relationship.

That will require a bit of work on your end. You'll need to spend some time thinking about how you want to divide and subdivide your relationships, then you'll need to create and populate all those different circles. Every day after that, you'll need to determine which posts go to which circles—and which circles you want to include in you daily stream reading.

As I said, a lot of work—to the goal of having your complex life perfectly organized, at least within the confines of Google+.

Examining Circle Strategies

I'm going to assume that you prefer some sort of multiple circle strategy. (If you instead prefer a two circle approach, just stop reading now and turn to the next chapter.) With that in mind, here are some circle strategies you may want to consider.

Organizing by Type of Friend

Not all friends are created equal. You probably have a small handful of friends for life—your very closest BFFs that you share every intimate detail of your life with. Then you have those folks you talk to regularly, but aren't really that close to. Then there are folks who are more like acquaintances than friends, you know them by name but aren't that interested in what they're doing. And there may even be "friends" who are further removed than that—what we might call "online friends," in that they're on your list but you really don't know them at all.

With this sort of friend segmentation a reality, why not create circles to mirror this sort of organization? That is, you create the following circles:

Best Friends. Your closest half-dozen or so pals.

Casual Friends. People you interact with on a regular basis but aren't that close to.

Neighbors. The folks in your neighborhood, who are kind of friends but not really.

Acquaintances. People you know but don't really care about.

Fake Friends. Everybody else on your friends list, even if you don't really know them personally.

GOOGLE+ PLUS

Don't worry about using potentially insulting names for your circles; your friends never see the circles they're in.

Organizing by Family Relationship

Just as not all friends are created equal, neither are all family members. In fact, if you belong to a rather large family, you know that you're closer to some family than to others.

With that in mind, here's a way to organize your family contacts into multiple circles:

Nuclear Family. Your spouse and kids—'nuff said.

Immediate Family. Your parents, grandparents, and siblings.

Extended Family. This is where you put crazy Uncle Walt and all your cousins, nephews, and what not—the folks you only interact with during family reunions.

Depending on how close you are to various family members, you may choose a different approach, with circles for cousins, nephews/nieces, aunts/uncles, and the like. It all depends on how you interact with whom.

Organizing by School Relationship

If you're a student, it makes sense to create a Classmates circle of some sort. But not all classmates are the same, and you can't forget about your teachers, either, so here's a circle strategy you may wish to employ:

Study Group. Your closest school friends—the folks you study with and depend on.

Classmates. Everybody else you go to school with.

Teachers. Not your classmates, but your teachers, teaching assistants, and so forth. (This way you can avoid sending embarrassing party pics to your professors.)

Former Classmates. Classmates from previous years.

Former Teachers. Old teachers you still want to keep in touch with.

You can also choose to create circles for the different classes you take, or for different subject areas. So you might have circles for Philosophy 101 and Accounting 302, or circles for Philosophy, Business, and the like.

Organizing by Work Relationship

Creating a Work circle, separate from a Friends circle, makes a lot of sense. But if you work in a larger company, chances are you have a complex web of relationships to manage. Here's one approach to doing so:

Team Workers. The people in your immediate team or department. For example, if you work in marketing, you would include everybody else in the marketing department.

Co-Workers. These are the folks at or near your level that you interact with every day.

Managers. Your boss and other managers near or at that level. Make sure not to send those complaining posts their way.

Senior Management. The big bosses. Be careful what you send them.

Fellow Employees. Everybody else who works there, whether you know them or not.

If your company has multiple locations, you can create circles for each office. You may also choose to create circles for each functional department—Marketing, Sales, Accounting, and so forth.

Placing your company within the context of a larger industry, you can also create a circle for Colleagues—people you know who work for similar firms. For that matter, if you're looking to change jobs in the near future, create a circle for Potential Employers—and make sure not to get your posts to this circle mixed up with your Managers circle.

Organizing by Eras

The older you get, the more friends you make. It's easy enough to group these friends into certain time periods, like this:

High School Friends. The folks you went to high school (or even grade school!) with.

College Friends. Your pals from college.

Adult Friends. Friendships you've made since graduating.

If you're married, maybe you need a circle for Couple Friends—friends you and your wife have made as a couple. And as you get older, you may find you want to segment your Adult Friends into additional eras—Young Adult Friends, Middle Aged Friends, Retirement Friends, and so forth.

GOOGLE+ PLUS

Alternatively, you can organize your friends by age rather than era. So you'd have circles for Under 21, 21-30, 31-40, and so forth.

Organizing by Interest

This one's easy. If you have any hobbies or non-work-related interests, create circles to keep in touch with the folks you interact with there.

For example, if you're into community theater, create a Community Theater circle and include all your acting buddies. If you're in the church choir, create a Church Choir circle and include fellow choir members. If you're a big fan of Doctor Who, create a Doctor Who circle and populate it with fellow fans of the Time Lord. You get the picture.

Along the same lines, if you belong to any type of community organization, it naturally makes sense to create a circle for that organization. In fact, you may need more than one circle; you can create a circle for Members, another for Financial Supporters, and so forth.

And if you or your children play sports, you can create circles for the various teams or leagues you're involved with. You can even create circles for Players, Coaches, Parents, Fans, and so forth.

Organizing for Musicians

Here's a special case. If you're a working musician or in a band, you can use circles to help segregate your fan base and the people you work with. Create the following circles:

Band. Just you and your band mates. Use this circle to discuss creative and scheduling issues.

Crew. This is for your roadies, sound team, and so forth—maybe even your accountant and lawyer.

Fans. Use this circle to connect with the bulk of your audience.

Supporters. These days many musicians are encouraging donations to help support their recording efforts. Give your financial supporters their own circle for privileged communications.

Media. Because you need to reach out to members of the music press.

Organizing by Geography

Sometimes the best organization is a geographic one. That is, create circles for Local Friends, Midwest Friends, West Coast Friends, and so on. In fact, you can employ this local focus to other types of organization—Midwest Co-Workers, European Fans of Doctor Who, and the like.

GOOGLE+ PLUS

The more circles you have, the harder it may be to keep track of them. You can better manage a large number of circles by giving them "nested" names, in which you subdivide major topics. For example, instead of using a single Friends circle, you may create circles for Friends: Work, Friends: College, Friends: High School, and so forth.

Creating a Sharing Circle

Beyond the circle strategies just discussed, sometimes you can't easily segment your friends and contacts using simple demographics. If you're like me, you probably find yourself sharing a whole lot with a select group of individuals that share no other defining feature other than you like to share with them. In this instance, you can create a circle—perhaps labeled Sharing—just for sharing with these folks.

The key here is to identify those individuals that you regularly communicate and share with, no matter what other circles they're a part of. Create your Sharing circle and place these folks in it. This Sharing circle can then be your default for all new posts and uploads.

Creating Circles for Your Other Social Network Friends

What about all the friends you have on Facebook and other social networks? How can you best use circles to share with them?

The most basic approach is to create circles for each social network. So you'd create a Facebook circle, a Twitter circle, a LinkedIn circle, and so forth, and then populate each circle with those friends who've migrated to Google+.

Of course, you can further segment these social network friends into sub-types—Facebook: Friends, Facebook: Family, Facebook: Classmates, and so forth. It all depends on how granular you want to get.

Using the Public Circle

Know that when you create a new Google+ post, you have the option of posting to Public. Now, "Public" isn't a circle per se; it simply indicates that the post can be searched and viewed by anyone on Google+.

When you're posting personal information, you don't want to select the Public option. It's better to be a little discreet about who you share things with.

But when you want to make a bigger splash, some sort of public pronouncement, then going Public makes sense. It's also a good option if you are or are representing a company, celebrity, or other public figure; you have to do a Public post to get promotional value from it.

So if you want your musings to be universally available, make sure you select Public in addition to whatever other circles you want. It's the only way to gain visibility with the entire Google+ base.

Creating Personal Circles

One last thing. You can use circles for your own personal benefit, without necessarily singling out other individuals as participants. That is, you can use circles to organize posts that you really like or want to read later—or to store drafts of your own future posts.

Creating a Favorites Circle

Let's start with using circles to store your favorite posts. Start by creating a circle labeled Favorites, but don't place anyone into that circle. When you find a post you really like, opt to share it with your Favorites circle. You can then display the Favorites stream to view all these posts you've informally "favorited."

Creating a Read Later Circle

Same thing with posts you don't have time to fully read at this point in time but want to read later. Create a circle labeled Read Later and don't add anyone to it. When you find a post worthy of future examination, share it to the Read Later circle. Later, you can display the Read Later stream and then read the posts within at your leisure.

Creating a Drafts Circle

You can also use this type of personal circle to hold drafts of posts you're not yet ready to post. This works when you create an empty circle labeled Drafts. Then, when you start composing a post but don't have time to finish it, share it with the Drafts circle. You can then go back and re-display the post, finish writing it, and send it on its way to other circles.

The Least You Need to Know

- As you start using Google+, you have to decide on whether you want to use a small number or large number of circles.
- You can employ different strategies for creating and naming circles; you don't have to settle for Google+'s default circles.
- Circles can also be used to store your favorite posts, as well as posts you want to read at a later date.

More Creative Uses for Hangouts

Chapter 21

In This Chapter

- Using hangouts to keep in touch with family members
- Using hangouts in a business environment
- Using hangouts for teaching and studying
- Using a hangout to create a video surveillance system

As you learned back in Chapter 11, a hangout is a group video chat on Google+. Each hangout can have up to 10 participants; all you need to join in is a computer with a webcam and a live internet connection.

That's all well and good, but what can you use hangouts for? There are actually a lot of creative uses for this innovative feature—as you'll soon learn.

Keeping in Touch with Family

Probably the most common use of video chat is to keep in touch with family while you're away from home. Now, you don't need hangouts to do this; in most instances, basic one-on-one video chat (such as that offered by Google+'s normal Chat feature) works just fine.

However, if you want to set up a family meeting with members scattered all around the country, creating a hangout is definitely in order. Consider if you have children who've moved away from home; you can hold a mini-family reunion any time you like, just by creating a hangout and inviting all the kids. For that matter, you can use a hangout to include family members who couldn't travel for a physical reunion; it doesn't matter where they are, as long as they have an internet connection.

Conducting Video Conferences and Meetings

In the business world, a hangout is terrific for holding video conferences, webinars, and other types of meetings. The rise of email, instant messaging, and social media may have led to a decline in interpersonal business communication, but Google+ Hangouts might change all that. With the ability to see up to 10 of your colleagues face-to-face, you may find that communication is improving.

With hangouts you don't need to fly people across country or drive them across town to put together a simple business meeting. You can talk in person, for as long as you like, with up to 10 of your colleagues, all for free.

The free part is nice for cost-conscious businesses. It's not that hangouts do anything you can't do with other video conferencing systems, it's that it does it for free. You don't need expensive equipment or online video conferencing services that can run into the thousands of dollars. Hangouts are free—assuming, of course, that everyone involved has a webcam connected to or built into their computer.

Businesses of all types and sizes can use a hangout for video conferencing. It's especially useful for businesses with a lot of telecommuters; now you can hold that weekly meeting without everyone having to travel into the office to attend.

Conducting Sales Calls

You may also find that hangouts are a good way to reduce your company's sales expenses. Instead of flying a sales rep and support personnel to a client, hold a hangout, instead. You get the one-on-one between your rep and the client, of course, but also have the option of plugging in personnel from other parts of the company as needed.

Hangouts are also good for calling on companies where multiple decision makers are involved. Instead of trying to line up multiple meetings with multiple influencers, your rep instead sets up a single hangout with the necessary folks at the client firm. One meeting, multiple influencers, good deal.

Servicing Clients

Your use of hangouts doesn't have to stop when you make the sale. You can use hangouts to keep clients up to speed on how a project is progressing.

The key thing to remember here is that a hangout stays open until the last participant checks out, even if no one is really doing anything on camera. You can open a hangout between your company and the client, keep it open, and then return to it when you have something to show. It's a live, continuous connection you can use in any way necessary.

Enhancing Customer Service

Thinking a little further outside the box, consider using hangouts as part of your customer service program. I'm not talking about one-on-one video chats between customer service reps and customers (although that's a good idea, you can do that with regular Google Chat), but rather something a little more ambitious.

Instead of one-on-one support chats, how about establishing video support groups? That is, have one of your customer service reps start a hangout, and then invite multiple customers to join in. As you find with web-based message forums, a group of customers are likely to answer their own questions without the need of official moderation. (Although that can be available, too.)

Conducting Customer Training

Moving beyond customer support, it's easy to see how you can use hangouts for after-the-sale customer training. If you need to instruct a group of employees how to use your product or service, just have them all log in to a hangout and start training. You can answer questions as they pop-up, and hold as many hangouts as you need to cover all of your client's users.

Conducting Board Meetings and Analyst Calls

If your company has investors, you can use hangouts to hold your quarterly or annual analyst calls. Just invite all the necessary financial analysts and then you can talk to them face-to-face—which is much more personal than the typical analyst telephone conferences.

For that matter, you can use a hangout to conduct your company's board meetings. You don't have to spend money flying board members in to attend; just invite the board to a hangout and let them talk as long as they want.

Holding Press Conferences

When your company wants to meet with select journalists, you no longer have to fly them in from across the country or conduct an impersonal teleconference. Instead, invite the preferred members of the media to a hangout; you can then make your announcement and accept questions face-to-face (to face) in real time.

One thing I like about using Google+ Hangouts for press conferences is how quickly you can set them up. Trying to schedule a traditional press conference can take days; even a pro-level teleconference can take hours to setup and send invitations. With a hangout, however, one email does the trick and you can be chatting within minutes. Fast and personal, a great way to manage the press.

Conducting Job Interviews

If you're like me, you hate the hiring process. Job interviews are time consuming, especially if you need multiple managers from throughout your organization to interview each applicant.

Instead, schedule a single hangout for each applicant. Invite each relevant department head or manager, and have the applicant talk to all of you as a group, or each of you consecutively. It's much more efficient than trying to do it physically.

Collaborating as a Group

Collaboration is a big thing. Whether you're collaborating with people in the same office, in different locations, or in completely different companies, hangouts can make the collaboration process that much easier.

All you need to do is start up a hangout for the project at hand, and invite all the key collaborators. Keep the hangout open, so anyone can jump in at any time. This lets you have individual face-to-face conversations, as well as group meetings for all collaborators.

This works, by the way, even outside the business world. You could be collaborating on a community project, a sports team, a family get together, or whatever. Hangouts are great for putting all your heads together to get a job done.

GOOGLE+ PLUS

You can also use hangouts for collaborating on creative projects. Consider musicians in a band, for example. Two or more band members can form a hangout to write a song; it's almost like being in the same room. Or if you're doing a recording project, with everybody contributing from different locations (which is pretty common these days), establishing a hangout provides the face-to-face interaction that might not be present, otherwise.

Performing Live

Musicians are finding hangouts useful for scheduling in-person performances for key supporters—folks who've provided backing money for recording projects, for example. With hangouts, you do your performing over the internet, to groups of 10 at a time. It's both intimate and efficient.

For that matter, you can use hangout concerts as perks or promotions for your fans. Have them register to win a prize, and have the prize be a live concert. You can give the concert to up to 10 prize winners.

You can also use hangouts to perform for the media. Schedule a hangout for a half-dozen or so of your key press contacts, then put on a show. It's more efficient than doing half a dozen press conferences all in a row.

Hosting Book Club Meetings and Bible Study Groups

Book clubs are big deals, with groups of a dozen or so readers getting together to discuss the chosen book; sometimes they even invite the author to phone in and comment. Well, now you don't have to worry about braving the elements, or dealing with members who live too far away to attend regularly. Just hold your book club meeting in a hangout, invite the author (through his or her publicist, of course), and hold your discussion as normal. It works surprisingly well.

And if hangouts work for book clubs, they also work for other forms of small, personal meetings, such as bible study groups. Again, you don't have to be there in person to attend, which should increase attendance. It's all about making it easier to meet through technology.

Conducting Neighborhood Meetings

Maybe you're a member of a neighborhood or condo association. Maybe you're just a concerned neighbor volunteering for the latest project. In any case, you can use hangouts to hold your neighborhood meetings, without anyone having to leave the comfort of their own houses.

This is similar in concept to company board meetings held via hangout. You may have to amend your bylaws to make sure video attendees count towards a quorum, but you'll probably get higher attendance than you would through traditional methods.

Teaching a Class

Online learning is getting bigger, and now you can conduct your classes using hangouts. It doesn't matter what you teach, you can talk into your webcam and get all instructional.

I think hangout classes are particularly useful for the small classes typical of community education. Imagine a cooking class held via hangout, for example, or any sort of crafts class. Heck, hangouts would be ideal for yoga and other personal training classes. The sky's the limit.

GOOGLE+ PLUS

You can even incorporate hangouts into the traditional classroom environment, to accommodate students who can't attend in person.

Hosting a Study Group

Speaking of students, the days of getting together to study for a test or work on a group project are so old school. Instead, students today can create hangouts for their study groups, and get together without leaving their dorm rooms.

Hangout study groups get even more interesting when you incorporate Google's other online tools. You can participate in side text chats within the hangouts window, of course, or use Gmail to send important files back and forth. There's a lot you can do online, without having to clutter up somebody's dorm room or living room.

Watching YouTube Videos—as a Group

As you recall from Chapter 11, you can play YouTube videos during a hangout. There are lots of both professional and personal uses for that feature.

On a professional level, you can incorporate YouTube videos in your business meetings, either for fun or function. For example, if your company has uploaded some training videos to YouTube, you can start up a hangout and then play the videos to the group.

On a personal level, it's always fun to get a group of friends together to watch TV shows, movies, and other videos. Now you don't have to be physically together to do so. Just set a time to get together, have your friends log in, and then start playing the video you want to watch. You can even talk to each other while the video plays, just like you were there.

Setting Up a Video Surveillance System

Here's an interesting personal use for hangouts that I'm not sure Google ever intended. You can set up a hangout on multiple computers to provide an "always on" video surveillance system for your home or small office.

This takes a bit of explaining and some time to set up, so bear with me here.

First, you'll need a webcam and computer set up at each location you want to monitor. Not a big deal, there, other than that you have to leave the computer on all the time.

Second, you'll need a separate Google+ account for each of these computers, as well as for your own computer you'll be watching things from.

With everything set up and turned on, you start a hangout from your main computer and account, then invite and log on all the other computers/accounts. You now have live streaming video from each computer you've set up; leave the hangout open and monitor each location as you like.

Once you have everything running, you can use your new surveillance system to monitor visitors who ring your door bell, check to see if packages have been delivered, check your aquarium while you're on vacation, or even monitor your kids while they sleep. The uses are almost endless.

GOOGLE+ PLUS

Since you can join a hangout from your smart phone, you don't even have to be near a computer to monitor your hangout-based surveillance system. It's easy enough to pull out your phone to see what's going on, even if you're having dinner at a fancy restaurant or driving down the interstate.

The Least You Need to Know

- Hangouts are great for keeping in touch with absent family members.
- There are many creative business uses for hangouts, including holding press conferences and conducting job interviews.
- Hangouts are also useful for enabling group collaboration, holding study groups, or teaching a small class.
- You can even create a hangout to use as a video surveillance system.

Using Google+ for Business

Chapter

22

In This Chapter

- Why Google+ makes sense for your business
- Learning about Google+ business profiles
- Using your personal profile to market your business on Google+
- Using Google's +1 button to improve your site's search rank

Social media marketing is the current big thing for many businesses. If you're doing any online marketing at all, chances are you've added Facebook and Twitter to your marketing mix.

Where, then, does Google+ fit into your online marketing strategy? There are lots of things you can do now and a lot more you'll be able to do in the future. (And that's on top of the non-marketing business uses of Google+, such as online collaboration and video conferences.)

Why Google+ Makes Sense for Business

Social media have proven quite useful for companies marketing their products and services online. In part that's because of the numbers of users involved, but it's also about the personal connections you can make with your customer base.

The numbers alone are compelling. Facebook has 750 million users, Twitter 200 million, and Google+ 20 million or so and growing rapidly. These are all potential customers. In fact, social media is so entrenched in society today that many of these users are probably your existing customers—and they may already be talking about you online.

And there's real benefit from having your customers talk about you on Google+, Facebook, or Twitter—especially if they link back to your website in their posts. Links are good in and of themselves because they generate traffic, but these inbound links also increase your site's ranking in Google's search results. That's because search ranking is at least partly dependent on the number of inbound links a site receives. The more often you're mentioned (or +1'd), the higher your site will rank with Google and other major search sites.

Another benefit to customers talking about you in social media is that it's good word-of-mouth marketing. As all marketers know, a strong word-of-mouth campaign trumps any form of paid advertising or promotion. It's quality attention, which results in quality traffic to your company's website.

There are also the connections you make in social media—that is, the relationships you build between your company and your customers. Social media, such as Google+, provide a unique opportunity to conduct ongoing conversations with your most loyal customers, which not only helps to cement customer ties but also provides valuable feedback about your company and products. When you get your customers involved with social media, they become more invested in your company; they feel like they're part of your team, participating in the day-to-day workings of your company and products.

Even better is the fact that all these benefits can accrue with minimal financial investment. When you're marketing on Google+ and other social networks, you don't have to buy expensive advertisements or otherwise spend a lot of big bucks; all you have to invest is your time. Spend the time participating in Google+ and Facebook conversations and you'll find you have a new and interactive internet presence that forms a tight bond between you and your customers.

To this end, many marketers have found great success interacting with customers on Facebook and Twitter. Well, Google+ is just the next target on this social media hit list—anything you can do, promotion-wise, on the other social networks, you ought to be able to do on Google+, too. Which is why many businesses are eying Google+ as a potential marketing vehicle.

GOOGLE+ INSIDER

Learn more about social media marketing in my book *The Ultimate Web Marketing Guide* (Que, 2010).

Waiting for Google+ Business Profiles

The most obvious way to get started marketing on Google+ would be to create a profile for your company or brand. The problem, at least during the initial launch stage, is that Google won't let you do that.

That's right, Google has so far been discouraging businesses from participating in Google+. Which is a bit of a bummer.

This initial constraint is entirely a factor of Google+ being a brand-new service. That is, during the initial launch, Google is reserving Google+ accounts for individuals only, and preventing businesses from creating accounts. Or, as Google+'s product manager, Christian Oestlien put it:

"Right now we're very much focused on optimizing for the consumer experience, but we have a great team of engineers building a similarly optimized business experience for Google+. We just ask for your patience while we build it. In the meantime, we are discouraging businesses from using regular profiles to connect with Google+ users. Our policy team will actively work with profile owners to shut down non-user profiles."

In other words, Google+ isn't ready for businesses yet, but they're working on it. In fact, by the time you read this book, it's likely that Google will have launched a variant of Google+ designed specifically for business use.

GOOGLE+ INSIDER

Google has hinted that the business version of Google+ would include "rich analytics and the ability to connect that identity to other parts of Google that businesses might use on a daily basis." That includes being able to use Google Offers to include online coupons and discounts; integrate a Google+ page with Google Analytics and Google AdWords; and list multiple locations via Google Maps and Places. It's likely that by the time you read this, this new service will already be available.

So what might a Google+ business profile look like? Well, Figure 22.1 shows a test page that Ford created for Google+. As you can see, it looks a lot like a normal personal profile page, but with more dominant company branding and product images. There's also an Add to Circles button that easily lets interested customers add this page to their circles (presumably their Following circle). Not surprisingly, the bulk of the page is a stream of company posts; the posts include normal text announcements, product photos, and videos.

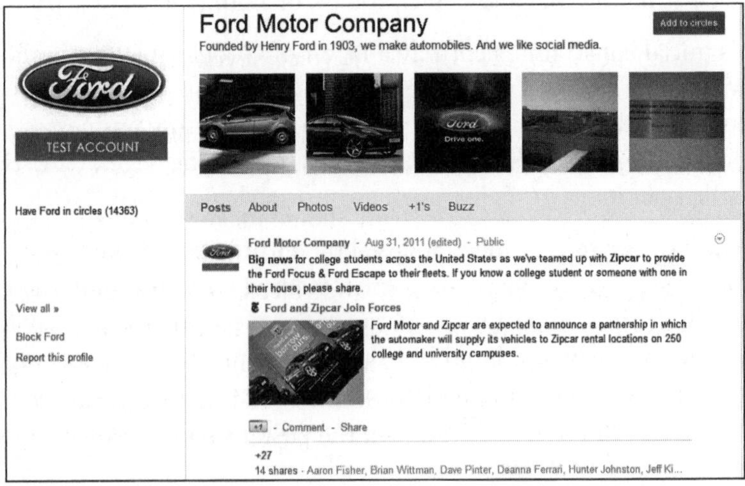

Figure 22.1: *Ford's test Google+ business profile.*

Unfortunately, though, you have to wait until Google rolls this out to all its users before you can create your own Google+ business profile. Until then … well, there are some other ways you can use Google+ for your business.

Using a Personal Profile for Your Business

Even though Google has said they're discouraging businesses using Google+ at all right now (and will, in fact, delete any business that sets up an account), many companies have found a way to use Google+'s to market their businesses. It's all about being creative with personal profiles.

What you want to do is assign one individual as your company or brand spokesperson. This person can then use his or her personal profile to market your business on Google+.

GOOGLE+ PLUS

It's important that the person you designate as your representative on Google+ have your company's official public approval. This person should also make sure to include your company as his employer in his Google+ profile, so anyone searching in that fashion will find him.

The key is to set this person up as the voice of your company. If he expresses suitable expertise (and the requisite social communications skills), he'll quickly build a following—a following not just for him individually, but also for your company and products.

This representative of your company should make the same types of posts as your company would otherwise. That means a steady stream of product announcements, photos, and videos, as well as any necessary industry news and information. It's important that whatever this person posts be of interest to current and potential customers—and be useful enough that it justifies customers' adding that person to their circles. All posts should reflect the poster's own personality, of course, but also hew the company line.

It's important that this person constantly monitor his Google+ presence. Followers will want to comment on his posts, as well as contact him directly with their won posts and messages. All of this is great customer interaction, but demands immediate attention. Social media is a two-way street, of course; that will require a sufficient investment in time and energy to fulfill the promise.

This interaction also means participating in other conversations on Google+, not just those on this person's profile page. To get the most out of Google+ (or any social network), you have to become an active member of the community. This means not only posting to his own profile, but also posting to other members of Google+. It's a great way to get the word out.

Of course, you'll need to promote your representative person's Google+ feed in other media, as well. That means including a link to this profile on your web page and blog, in your promotional email messages, in your online and print ads, even in your existing social media (Facebook and Twitter feeds).

You'll also need to devise some mechanism for customers to give their Google+ usernames or email addresses to your representative on Google+. That's because you need to add your customers to your circles—it doesn't really work the other way around. In fact, you may end up creating multiple circles for different brands or product lines, and then filtering your communications to different circles accordingly.

Other Ways You Can Use Google+ for Your Business

Social media like Google+ aren't just for outbound marketing. You can also utilize Google+ for other business purposes. All it takes is a little creativity.

Using Chat and Hangouts for Internal Communication and Collaboration

One obvious use of Google+ is to use text chat and video hangouts to facilitate internal communications within your company. Both these features make for quick and easy communication between employees, whether they're in the same office or located a continent apart. And it's not just for communication; hangouts, especially, are great for group collaboration (refer to Chapter 21 for more). Use these tools at your disposal—they're free.

Hosting Hangouts for Customers

Hangouts are also useful for communicating with current and potential customers. You can use hangouts to host webinars, provide customer service and support, deliver product training, and more. It's a great way to establish face-to-face communication with your customers—without anyone incurring undue travel expense.

Considering the +1 Button

There's one last aspect of Google+ that may bear interest to many businesses. It has to do with Google's +1 button—and its impact on your company's search ranking.

You should be familiar with the +1 button found on many websites (and shown in Figure 22.2). It's Google's way of letting users "like" or recommend a given web page, blog post, or article.

Figure 22.2: *Google's +1 button.*

The +1 button will probably directly impact search engine optimization (SEO)—but it's not yet exactly clear how.

Now here's where things get interesting. If you're signed in to Google and start a search, the search results may include the names of your online friends who've +1'd a given page. If none of your friends has +1'd a page, the result may still display the aggregate number of +1s that page has received from all users.

In addition, +1s from your friends may also affect how a site ranks when you search. That's because Google figures that content recommended by friends is more relevant than content from strangers. So if some of your friends have +1'd a given page, that page may rank higher in the results when you conduct a search.

It's also possible (probable, really) that Google will start incorporating +1s into its overall web search rankings. It's easy to imagine a scenario where the more +1's a given page receives across the board (not just from friends), the higher that page will rank in Google's search results.

To that end, you need to consider the +1 button as part of your search engine optimization efforts. The first step to take is to add +1 buttons to your website and to each individual blog post (if you have a company blog). You can do this by going to www.google.com/webmasters/+1/button/ and following the instructions there.

Beyond this, you should begin encouraging visitors to +1 your page and posts, much the same way you encourage visitors to "like" your page on Facebook. The more people you actively recommend what you're doing, however they do it, will improve your search ranking—and increase future traffic to your site.

The Least You Need to Know

- Google+, like all social media, helps you reach new customers and establish closer relationships with existing customers.
- During the initial launch, Google+ does not allow business profiles—although that's bound to change.
- Until you can create a business profile, you can use your personal profile to establish yourself as your company's official representative on Google+.
- You can also use Google+ to facilitate internal communication and collaboration and host video conferences and training for your customers.
- Add Google's +1 button to your website and blog posts to improve your site's search ranking.

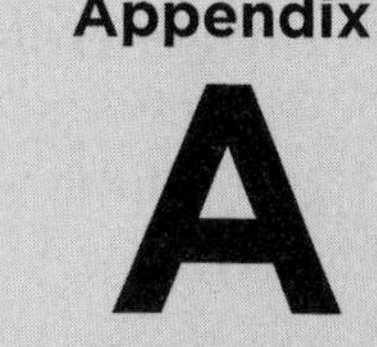

Appendix A

Glossary

+1 button An icon, supported by Google, that enables users to "like" or recommend a given web page.

AdWords Google's advertising network that places context-sensitive ads on Google search results pages and other sites.

blog A kind of online diary.

Chat Google+'s real-time text-based instant messaging service.

circle A grouping of Google+ friends according to some defined criteria.

conversation A text chat initated with Google+ Messenger.

email Short for "electronic mail," a way to send messages electronically over the internet.

extension An add-on to a web browser that introduces a specific function to the browser.

Facebook Currently the web's largest social network.

friend Someone you interact with on a social network.

Friendster The web's first social network, launched in 2002.

geotagging The process of adding geographical information to selected items, such as message posts or digital photos.

Google Account An individual user account that signs you into all of Google's services, including Google+.

Google Buzz A social messaging tool, integrated into Google's Gmail service.

Google navigation bar A black bar that appears at the top of all Google pages—the Google search page, Google Calendar, Google+, and so forth—and offers direct access to many popular Google services.

Google Wave An ill-fated social messaging service launched by Google in 2010—and killed the same year.

Google+ Google's newest social network, offering message posting, photo and video sharing, instant messaging, and more.

Google+ profile Personal information in a public format on the Google+ site; typically contains information about who you are and what you like.

GPS Short for Global Positioning System, a worldwide navigational service enabled by satellite technology.

Hangouts Google+'s multi-user video chat service.

instant messaging A type of real-time, text-based communication between two or more computer users.

Light Tray The photo viewing pane used in Google+.

LinkedIn A social network targeted at business professionals.

media sharing sites Online communities where users can share digital photos, videos, and the like.

Messenger Google+'s group chat service for mobile phone users.

metadata Information that describes the contents of a file, such as a digital photo.

microblogging services Web-based services that let users broadcast short text messages across the internet.

MySpace A social network, launched in 2003, that for a period of time was the largest social network on the web.

orkut Google's first social network, launched in 2004 but never gained much traction in the United States.

photo album A means of storing multiple photos in a single location, such as a folder for photos.

Picasa Web Albums Also known as Google Photos, Google's online photo-sharing service, also tied into Google+.

post A short text message shared on the Google+ site.

resolution A measure of the amount of detail in a picture.

seekbar On YouTube, the bar underneath the video player that lets viewers skip directly to a specific point in a video.

social bookmarking services Online services that let users bookmark and share their favorite web pages with others.

social games Online games with social elements—such as the ability to play against other users of a social network.

social media Various online sites and services used to share information, opinions, and experiences.

social network A web-based community that facilitates the sharing of information and experiences between online friends.

Sparks Trending content on the web.

story Within Google+, an item (typically a web page or article) found in the spark stream.

Stream Where posts from Google+ friends are displayed.

tag A means of identifying a specific individual in a photo.

text messaging A way to send short text messages via mobile phones.

Twitter The internet's largest microblogging service, where users "tweet" short (140-character) text messages.

video conference A real-time video meeting between two or more participants.

virtual worlds Gamelike graphic environments that mimic many of the same community features found in traditional social networks.

Appendix B

Google+ Shortcut Keys

Shortcut Key	Function
Spacebar	Scroll down the stream
Shift+Space	Scroll up the stream
J	Scroll down one post in stream
K	Scroll up one post in stream
Enter	Open comment box
Tab+Enter	Post comment
+ or @	Mention a person in a post

Index

Symbols

A

B

C

D

E

F

G

H

J-K-L

M

N

O

P–Q

R

S

T

U

V

W-X

Y-Z